The Myth Of The Descent Into Hades

Jane Ellen Harrison

Kessinger Publishing's Rare Reprints

Thousands of Scarce and Hard-to-Find Books on These and other Subjects!

- Americana
- Ancient Mysteries
- Animals
- Anthropology
- Architecture
- Arts
- Astrology
- Bibliographies
- Biographies & Memoirs
- Body, Mind & Spirit
- Business & Investing
- Children & Young Adult
- Collectibles
- Comparative Religions
- Crafts & Hobbies
- Earth Sciences
- Education
- Ephemera
- Fiction
- Folklore
- Geography
- Health & Diet
- History
- Hobbies & Leisure
- Humor
- Illustrated Books
- Language & Culture
- Law
- Life Sciences
- Literature
- Medicine & Pharmacy
- Metaphysical
- Music
- Mystery & Crime
- Mythology
- Natural History
- Outdoor & Nature
- Philosophy
- Poetry
- Political Science
- Science
- Psychiatry & Psychology
- Reference
- Religion & Spiritualism
- Rhetoric
- Sacred Books
- Science Fiction
- Science & Technology
- Self-Help
- Social Sciences
- Symbolism
- Theatre & Drama
- Theology
- Travel & Explorations
- War & Military
- Women
- Yoga
- *Plus Much More!*

We kindly invite you to view our catalog list at:
http://www.kessinger.net

THIS ARTICLE WAS EXTRACTED FROM THE BOOK:

Myths of the Odyssey in Art and Literature

BY THIS AUTHOR:

Jane Ellen Harrison

ISBN 0766190676

READ MORE ABOUT THE BOOK AT OUR WEB SITE:

http://www.kessinger.net

OR ORDER THE COMPLETE
BOOK FROM YOUR FAVORITE STORE

ISBN 0766190676

IV

THE MYTH OF THE DESCENT INTO HADES

WE have seen how strangely, in the Homeric conception of Circe, good and evil are intermingled; how at one time she seems a power of the baser sort, the lower world—a sinister demon luring body and soul to destruction by the bait of sense temptation; at another moment she is in very truth the daughter of Helios, the sun god, a goddess of light and strength, of comfort and new life. Towards the end of the story the shadows clear wholly away, and about the lady Circe is shed a radiancy of awful brightness—fitting portent of the dread experience to come. One seems to feel that, after the interlude of soft delight and feasting, needful for a while to repair the wasting of soul and body, there comes with fresh fitness a girding-up of spirit for new perils of yet more fearful import. The strain to come justifies beforehand a timely slacking of the tension. It was fitting that "for the full circle of a year" the battered mariners should "sit day by day feasting on abundant flesh and sweet wine." It was no less fitting that as "the seasons returned and the months wore away" their spirit should be "eager to be gone." The goddess never seems stronger and fairer than when to the entreaty of the hero she makes answer—

"Son of Laertes, of the seed of Zeus, Odysseus of many devices, tarry ye now no longer in my house against your will; but first must ye perform another journey, and reach the dwelling of Hades and of dread Persephone, to seek to the spirit of Theban Teiresias, the blind soothsayer, whose wits abide steadfast. To him Persephone hath given judgment, even in death, that he alone should have understanding; but the other souls sweep shadow-like around."[1]

How much of help and strength from the goddess the human, childlike hero needed, we feel when he tells us—

"Thus spake she; but as for me, my heart was broken, and I wept as I sat upon the bed, and my soul had no more care to live and to see the sunlight. But when I had my fill of weeping and grovelling, then at the last I answered and spake unto her, saying, And who, Circe, will guide us on this way? for no man ever yet sailed to hell in a black ship."

The goddess may have smiled to herself at this feeble subterfuge, but her answering words are full of gracious comfort. "Son of Laertes, of the seed of Zeus, Odysseus of many devices, nay, trouble not thyself for want of a guide, by thy ship abiding; but set up the mast and spread abroad the white sails, and sit thee down, and the breeze of the north wind will bear thy vessel on her way." More than once we notice that when any great issue is to be accomplished, Odysseus, the crafty schemer, the man of "many a shift," is for a while helpless in the hands of the gods. Perhaps the most pathetic passage in the whole poem tells us how, fast asleep, he was borne by the Phæacians at last to his desired haven. "Soon as they

[1] *Od.* x. 486, etc.

MYTH OF THE DESCENT INTO HADES. 95

bent backwards and tossed the sea water with the oar-blade, a deep sleep fell upon his eyelids—a sound sleep, very sweet, and next akin to death." Thus did the black ship bear to his home "a man whose counsel was as the counsel of the gods, one that erewhile had suffered much sorrow of heart in passing through the wars of men, and the grievous waves; *but for that time he slept in peace,* forgetful of all that he had suffered."[1] So now, when he is bidden to fare to Hades, it is the goddess who sends in the wake of the ship a "welcome breeze;" the hero's strength is to sit still.

Circe tells him beforehand to what manner of land he will come, and we must follow closely her description, for nearly every detail we shall recognise again in some artistic portrayal of the under world.

"But when thou hast now sailed in thy ship across the stream Oceanus, where is a waste shore and the groves of Persephone, even tall poplar trees and willows that shed their fruit before the season, there beach thy ship by deep eddying Oceanus, but go thyself to the dark house of Hades. Thereby into Acheron flows Pyriphlegethon, and likewise Cocytus, a branch of the water of the Styx, and there is a rock, and a meeting of the two roaring waters." Precisely this picture we shall see figured on a Greek wall-painting, but before we turn to it we must hear to the end the monition of Circe.

[1] " καὶ τῷ νήδυμος ὕπνος ἐπὶ βλεφάροισιν ἔπιπτεν,
νήγρετος, ἥδιστος, θανάτῳ ἄγχιστα ἐοικώς.
. . . .
ἄνδρα φέρουσα θεοῖς ἐναλίγκια μήδε' ἔχοντα,
ὃς πρὶν μὲν μάλα πολλὰ πάθ' ἄλγεα ὃν κατὰ θυμόν,
ἀνδρῶν τε πτολέμους ἀλεγεινά τε κύματα πείρων
δὴ τότε γ' ἀτρέμας εὗδε, λελασμένος ὅσσ' ἐπεπόνθειν."
Od. xiii. 79-92.

"So, hero, draw nigh thereto, as I command thee, and dig a trench as it were a cubit in length and breadth, and about it pour a drink-offering to all the dead, first with mead, and thereafter with sweet wine, and for the third time with water, and sprinkle white meal thereon, and entreat with many prayers the strengthless heads of the dead, and promise that on thy return to Ithaca thou wilt offer in thy halls a barren heifer, the best thou hast, and wilt fill the pyre with treasure, and wilt sacrifice apart to Teiresias alone a black ram without spot, the fairest of your flock. But when thou hast with prayers made supplication to the lordly races of the dead, then offer up a ram and a black ewe, bending their heads towards Erebus, and thyself turn thy back, with thy face set for the shore of the river; then will many spirits come to thee of the dead that be departed. Thereafter thou shalt call to thy company and command them to flay the sheep which even now lie slain by the pitiless sword, and to consume them with fire; and to make prayer to the gods, to mighty Hades and to dread Persephone. And thyself draw the sharp sword from thy thigh and sit there, suffering not the strengthless heads of the dead to draw nigh to the blood, ere thou hast word of Teiresias. Then the seer will come to thee quickly, leader of the people; he will surely declare to thee the way and the measure of thy path, and as touching thy returning how thou mayest go over the teeming deep."

As the lady Circe ceased to speak the morning dawned, and she clad her hero in a mantle and doublet meet for the journey; and herself she arrayed in "a great shining robe, light of woof and gracious, and about her waist she cast a fair golden girdle, and put a veil upon her head."

Not in vain had been his sojourn in the magic halls, for straightway, from the transfigured presence of his divine mistress Odysseus passed out, and uproused his men, saying, "Sleep ye now no more, nor breathe sweet slumber; but let us go on our way, for the lady Circe hath verily shown me all."

We know what is to befall Odysseus; the time has come when he, like the hero of many another mythology, must descend into Hades. This is the uttermost trial by which the steadfast soul must be put to the proof. Only the great-hearted, even among the Greeks, might endure to the end: Dionysos to redeem his mother Semele; Herakles at the bidding of Eurystheus; Orpheus for his great love to Eurydike. It may be that these stories took their rise in some nature-myth; men saw the sun-god descend that he might ascend; but surely from very early days, about this simple notion there must have been woven a complex web of keen sorrow and vague aspiration—a longing, swiftly changed to a conviction, that somewhere, by some desolate lake or darkly yawning cavern, a way led to the world below, by which the living might pass to revisit the dead, the dead the living. How else should the Greeks have their Cimmerian land for Odysseus; the Romans their Avernus for Æneas; the Teutons their swamps of Drömling, whither departed souls have access; the Kelts their island on Lough Derg, sacred still as St. Patrick's Purgatory; the Aztecs their subterranean temple Michtan, door to the lower world; South African savages their cavern Marimatle, whence ghosts creep out, and whereby dead men's souls go down; Egyptians their sacred lake, across which the dead are rowed to their last home; Fijians their " calm and solemn place of cliff and forest, where the souls of the dead embark for the judgment-seat of Udengei, and whither the living come in pilgrimage, thinking to see ghosts and gods?"[1]

Not all nations, perhaps, are quick to fashion beautiful nature-myths; but all can feel the pang of separation from their dead, the desire for reunion. Among most there is also the feeling that to the dead, with their added experience, comes increase of wisdom,—wisdom to which, under specified conditions, they are willing to give oracular utterance, sometimes with beneficent, sometimes with malignant intent. Hence, beginning for the Greeks with the Theban Teiresias, we have the long line of traditions respecting magical rites and oracular utterances from the dead (νέκυια or νεκυομαντεῖα),—traditions dating from the dim distance of the Egyptian and Chaldæan past, through the classical period of Greece and Rome, through the legends of mediæval tribes, down in unbroken line to the latest manifestation of so-called spiritualistic phenomena,—a tradition sometimes degraded into a superstitious belief in possession by demons, sometimes sublimated into faith in the ministry of angels. In one and every modification we find this common formative element,—regret for the past shaping itself into comfort for the present, hope for the future.

It is happily not our duty to investigate these manifold νεκυομαντεῖα, to follow the clue of this golden thread of Truth, this faith in things invisible, through the maze of jugglery and deceit in which time has tangled it. For us there is a lighter and pleasanter task, though withal a solemn one,—to fare down into Hades with Odysseus, and reverently face the shade of the Theban Teiresias.

[1] Tylor, *Hist. of Primitive Cults.*

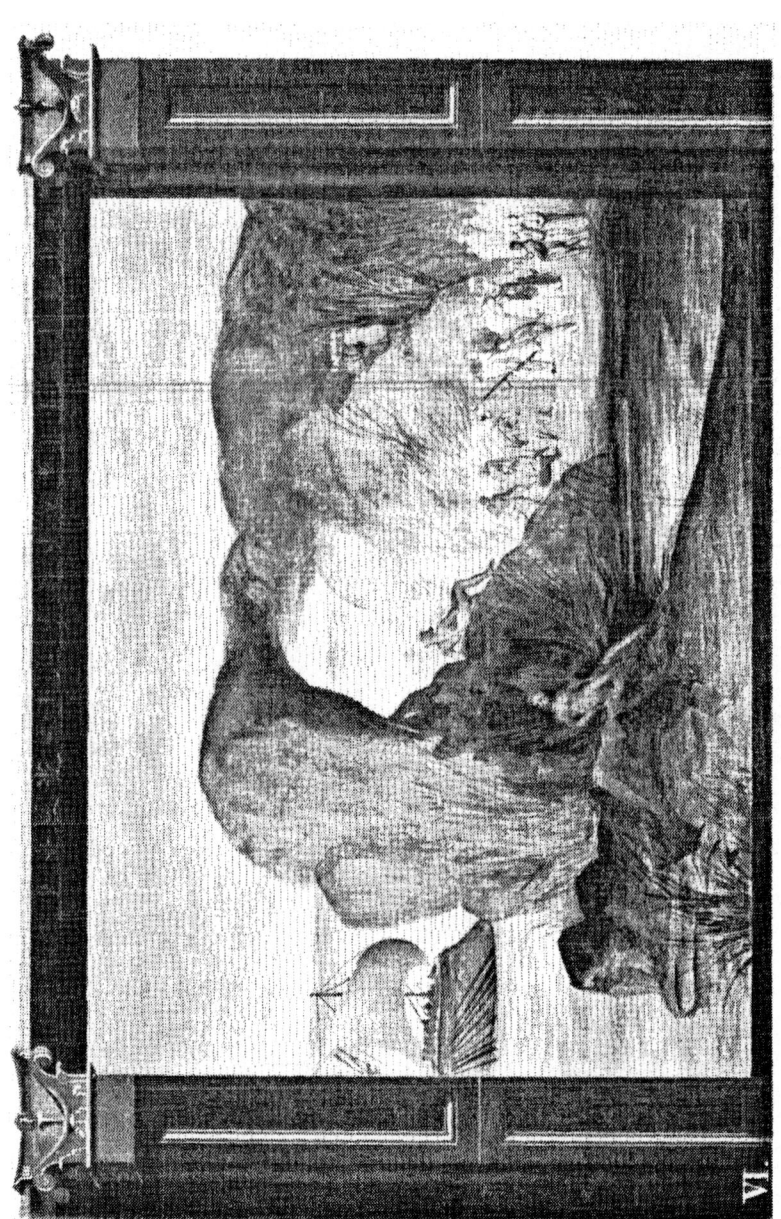

"Now when we had gone down to the ship and to the sea, first of all we drew the ship unto the fair salt water, and placed the mast and sails in the black ship, and took those sheep and put them therein; and ourselves too climbed on board, sorrowing, and shedding big tears. And in the wake of our darked-prowed ship she sent a favouring wind that filled the sails—a kindly escort—even Circe of the braided tresses, a dread goddess of human speech. And we set in order all the gear throughout the ship, and sat us down; and the wind and the helmsman guided our bark. And all day long her sails were stretched in her seafaring, and the sun sank, and all the ways were darkened.

"She came to the limits of the world, to the deep-flowing Oceanus. There is the land and the city of the Cimmerians, shrouded in mist and cloud, and never does the shining sun look down on them with his rays, neither when he climbs up the starry heavens, nor when again he turns earthward from the firmament, but deadly night is outspread over miserable mortals. Thither we came and ran the ship ashore, and took out the sheep; but for our part we held on our way along the stream of Oceanus till we came to the place which Circe had declared to us."[1] Such a place is before us in Autotype VI. (the sixth in our series of Odyssey landscapes). There is nothing very distinctively Greek about the scene; we might be looking at the Fijian "calm and solemn peace of cliff and forest;" we might be about to land on the sacred island in Lough Derg; we might be in Finland, the "home of the dreamy imagination, with its deep bays and inlets, its granite mountains," waiting for the hero Wainamoinen to descend into the

[1] *Od.* xi. 1, etc.

Finnish Hades. A consecrated calm rests upon the Homeric Hades both in the poet's words and in the painter's picture. In striking contrast is the description by Apollonius Rhodius[1] of the approach to Acheron; in the Hades he tells us the peaceful cliffs are sharp precipices, the quiet waters rage and swell, the wicked are like a troubled sea that cannot rest.

The Esquiline landscape is purely ideal—no sketch from the coastland by Cumæ. It is, however, strictly Homeric, the entrance to the under world such as Circe foretold.[2] To the left, on deep eddying Oceanus, still in full sail, is the ship of Odysseus (all the rest were destroyed by the Læstrygonians). It has not yet been drawn in to shore, probably the hero is still supposed to be on board. He is coming, indeed, to a "waste shore," a land "shrouded in mist and darkness." Very skilfully, and with a surprising mastery of chiaroscuro, the painter has thrown the whole of the right half into deep shadow, illumined only by light which streams in from the outer world through the rocky doorway. In the front are the steel-blue waters of Acheron, and watching beside these waters and those of the mighty Cocytus we are no longer surprised to see

---

[1] "ἢ μέν τε κρημνοῖσιν ἀνίσχεται ἠλιβάτοισιν
εἰς ἅλα δερκομένη Βιθυνίδα· τῇ δ' ὑπὸ πέτραι
λισσάδες ἐρρίζωνται ἁλίβροχοι· ἀμφὶ δὲ τῇσιν
κῦμα κυλινδόμενον μεγάλα βρέμει."

APOLL. RHOD. ii. 731-734.

[2] "ἀλλ' ὁπότ' ἂν δὴ νηὶ δι' Ὠκεανοῖο περήσῃς,
ἔνθ' ἀκτή τε λάχεια καὶ ἄλσεα Περσεφονείης
μακραί τ' αἴγειροι καὶ ἰτέαι ὠλεσίκαρποι
. . . . .
ἔνθα μὲν εἰς Ἀχέροντα Πυριφλεγέθων τε ῥέουσι
Κώκυτός θ' ὃς δὴ Στυγὸς ὕδατός ἐστιν ἀπορρώξ,
πέτρη τε ξύνεσίς τε δύω ποταμῶν ἐριδούπων."—Od. x. 508-515.

the personified rivers themselves. The whole scene is thickly overgrown with rushes; these are the sole representatives of the "tall poplar trees and willows that shed their fruit before the season," and they well serve to indicate the "waste," squalid shore. We shall see hereafter that these rushes may have been suggested by an older picture of greater fame. The main action of the scene takes place among the figures grouped to the right; but before we consider them we have other art monuments to review which deal with intermediate scenes, and we must advance a step further with the story.

"There Perimedes and Eurylochus held the victims; but I drew my sharp sword from my thigh, and dug a pit, as it were a cubit in length and breadth, and about it poured a drink offering to all the dead, first with mead and thereafter with sweet wine, and for the third time with water. . . . But when I had besought the tribes of the dead with vows and prayers, I took the sheep and cut their throats over a trench, and the dark blood flowed forth; and lo, the spirits of the dead that be departed gathered them from out of Erebus. Brides and youths unwed, and old men of many and evil days, and tender maidens with grief yet fresh at heart . . . and these many ghosts flocked together from every side about the trench with a wondrous cry, and pale fear got hold on me. . . . And myself I drew the sharp sword from my thigh, and sat there, suffering not the strengthless heads of the dead to draw nigh to the blood ere I had word of Teiresias."[1]

This piteous throng of waiting, eager ghosts we see pictured to the right of the scene in Autotype VI. Only

[1] *Od.* xi. 23, etc.

one will Odysseus allow to approach "ere" he has "word of Teiresias,"—his lost comrade Elpenor, who, though he has left the land of the living, still, because he lacks burial, has no lot as yet in the habitation of the dead. We see him seated high up on a rock (in Autotype VI.), away from the thronging ghosts; for though he has had speech with Odysseus, and due burial is promised, as yet his corpse lies still in the hall of Circe, dishonoured, unwept. His head is resting on his hand as if in sad meditation; above is the inscription Elpenor (ΕΛΠΗΝΩΡ); the E and the Ω are both defaced, the rest is clear; were there any doubt, the solitary position of the figure would suffice.

After Elpenor, had come up the soul of the mother of Odysseus; but even she is turned back to wait for the coming of the prophet. There is no figure in our picture inscribed Anticleia, but probably a woman standing to the front, behind Teiresias, is intended for her. "Anon came the soul of Theban Teiresias, with a golden sceptre in his hand, and he knew me and spake unto me: Son of Laertes, of the seed of Zeus, Odysseus of many devices, what seekest thou *now*, wretched man, wherefore hast thou left the sunlight and come hither to behold the dead and a land desolate of joy? Nay, hold off from the ditch and draw back thy sharp sword, that I may drink of the blood and tell thee sooth.

"So spake he, and I put up my silver-studded sword into the sheath, and when he had drunk the dark blood, even then did the noble seer speak unto me."[1]

This is probably the precise moment seized by the painter. The shades have trooped up, but are refused

[1] *Od.* xi. 88.

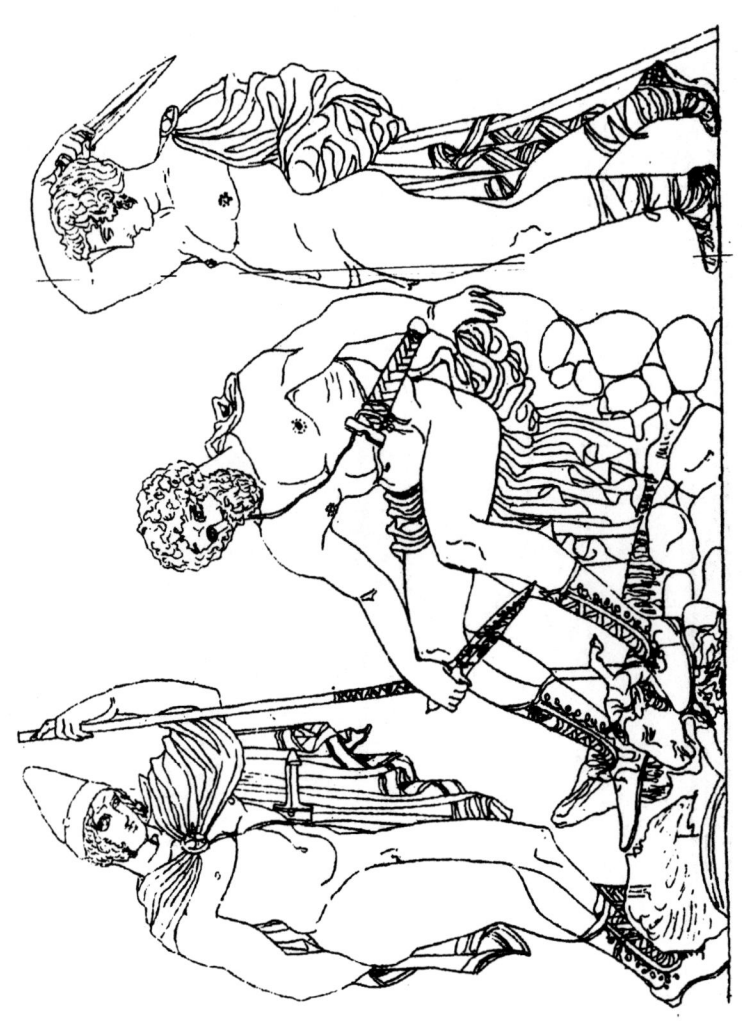

access; only Elpenor has had speech with Odysseus and returned to his rock. Teiresias approaches, a gray-bearded old man, clad in a long, priestly garment, a golden staff in his hand. Only one letter, the first of the inscribed name, is lost. Odysseus stands opposite in a curious attitude of eager expectancy; his inscription is quite clear (ΟΔΥΣΣΕΥΣ). Behind him to the left is the scene of the sacrifice. The ram lies dead on his back; Perimedes and Eurylochus are busy about him. Perimedes is clearly the figure most to the left, for though his inscription is gone, that of the other, Eurylochus, is still plain. We shall have to return to our picture again when the souls of the dead fair women come forward; but for the present we must turn to other works of art which deal with the oracle scene.

In Plate 27 we have a design from a vase, executed, to judge from the style, some time during the period of the Diadochi. In the centre of the picture Odysseus is seated on a heap of stones, rudely piled together, and covered by a hanging drapery. A chlamys falls loosely behind him, and he wears richly decorated buskins. His sword, also richly ornamented, has been drawn from the scabbard; he points it downward, and sits in an attitude of expectation; he wears neither helmet nor pilos. To the right stands a young man in similar dress; his right arm is cast over his head in a somewhat sensational attitude. To the left a second youth, wearing chlamys and pilos, leans in an easy attitude on his lance. The two side figures are presumably Eurylochus and Perimedes. At the feet of Odysseus we see the heads of the "ram and black ewe," the gift of Circe, newly slaughtered, and uprising from the trench is the ghost-like head of the seer Teiresias. The portrayal is very faithful to Homer; we have the pit, "as it were a cubit in length and breadth," the prescribed sacrifice, the seated hero, the drawn sword, the attendant comrades.[1] The design is executed in a large bold way, showing great mastery of outline, but already we miss something of the severity and simplicity of the old style. The attitudes and faces of all three figures are a little too elaborately expressive, the drapery too complex and sinuous, and the ornamentation on the buskins and weapons contrasts too emphatically with the simple naked forms. It is the design of an artist who worked under the influence rather of the traditions of painting than sculpture.

It is noticeable that nowhere does Homer specify the manner of the coming of Teiresias, so that the artist is left fancy-free in his depiction of the ghost's advent. His choice in this particular design is certainly curious. It is but fair to add that, mainly owing to the strange ghost head, grave doubt has been thrown on the whole portrayal. It has been maintained,[2] though I think without sufficient reason, that the head of Teiresias is interpolated, and that the scene depicted is not the descent into Hades at all. Take away this head, and we do not need to be told what would then be the natural interpretation: the mighty, seated hero and the slaughtered sheep would be enough. The doubt, though I believe it to be needless, is worth noting, because it reminds us of the extreme caution neces-

[1] "ἔνθ' ἱερήϊα μὲν Περιμήδης Εὐρύλοχός τε
ἔσχον· . . . .
βόθρον ὄρυξ' ὅσσον τε πυγούσιον ἔνθα καὶ ἔνθα . . . .
αὐτὸς δὲ ξίφος ὀξὺ ἐρυσσάμενος παρὰ μηροῦ
ἥμην."—*Od.* xi. 22 *seq.*

[2] On this question see Welcker, *Alte Denkmäler erklärt*, Part III.

sary in the interpretation of vases, and the ease with which a preconception may mislead. If we conceive the hero to be Odysseus, we interpret his attitude to be one of eager expectation; if Aias, of deep dejection. The moralist may note with satisfaction that nowhere more swiftly than in the study of archæology does the retribution of a false deduction follow on the error of a rash hypothesis.

Turning to Plate 28 we see a much more commonplace presentation of Teiresias. There is very little of the ghost about the old man leaning, half-seated, upon the rock, and conversing in serious ease with the hero opposite him. His character of seer is, however, indicated by the long garment, staff, and most of all by the veiled head. Odysseus stands opposite, his sword drawn; but his whole attitude, though perhaps not his face, is placid, almost careless; his foot is raised on a rock, and he rests his elbow on his knee; the descent into Hades is no doubt indicated by the rocky cleft which forms the background. The design is from a marble relief, now in the Louvre.

Of very curious and special interest is our next monument, relating to the Teiresias scene. We are not perhaps justified in calling it strictly Homeric, but it is certainly Odyssean. The design is from an Etruscan mirror (Plate 29); the execution is unusually careful and delicate. The seated figure is unmistakeably Odysseus. He is naked but for the drapery across his hip; he has drawn his sword, and points the blade upwards. The inscription is of course Etruscan, Uthuche, the frequent form for Odysseus. Equally unmistakeable is the standing figure; the winged petasos marks him at once as Hermes; his inscription would not help us much, Turms Aitas,—the letters read backwards. He lifts his hand as if speaking to Odysseus, no doubt introducing his companion. This strange companion chains our attention from the first glance. Looking at the faint drooping figure, so tenderly supported by the spirit guide, one thinks instantly of the "lady mother" of Odysseus, sorrow-worn Anticleia, who died because of her "sore longing" for her son; and Hermes seems for a moment the old-world prototype of the Apostle John. But alas it is not so! We are bound to read the at best mysterious inscription above the head of the drooping ghost, "Phinthial Teiresias." What Phinthial may mean is known to the Etruscans, and probably to them only; but the "Teiresias" is enough to dispel our pleasant fancy. It is the aged seer again; his eyes are closed, for he is blind; leaning on his staff, for he is old; softly shod, for he has come in silence from the under world.[1] So womanly is the figure that some critics have thought an allusion was intended to the current legend of the alternate sex of the prophet.[2] This does not seem probable. It is well known that the Greeks, with characteristic daring, did venture on the pourtrayal of a double sex. Ill brooking the wise dualism of nature, they imperiously demanded of art that she should adventure a unity more complete. But here we have, I think, no Hermaphroditic conception. This dim, feeble figure is rather a most fit presentation of the haggard, nervous *medium*, whose "sinews," in Greek phraseology, "no more

---

[1] One is reminded of the "hellshoon" (helsko), which the Norseman bound on the feet of his dead in forethought for the toilsome, downward road. These low flat shoes, however, occur not infrequently in Etruscan designs, and with no special import.

[2] Ovid's unprofitable account of this matter may be read in *Metam.* iii. 320, *sqq.*

Pl. 29.

bind together the flesh and the bones." It is not the image of a prophet such as Circe must have pictured when she bade Odysseus "seek to the spirit of Theban Teiresias, the blind soothsayer, *whose wits abide steadfast*."[1]

We must return for a moment to the guide of Teiresias. In the Odyssey story no Hermes is present at this particular crisis of the descent into Hades. The ghosts come up unmarshalled. Hermes' psychopompos or psychagogos is not, however, wholly un-Homeric; we find him later ushering down into the lower world the souls of the slain suitors.[2] Certainly Teiresias in our mirror-design looks most unlikely to have come by himself. Probably the whole conception embodied in this particular picture is due to some Etruscan version of the myth, which may in its turn have been borrowed from the lost tragedy of Æschylus, the *Psychagogoi*, in which Hermes figured,[3] though exactly in what capacity we do not know, and in which Teiresias is summoned, and gives utterance to a strange prophecy, which we shall soon have to consider. We must leave this dreamy Etruscan ghost, and listen to the fateful words which fell from the lips of the Homeric Teiresias, the shade "whose wits abide steadfast."

"Thou art asking of thy sweet returning, great Odysseus, but that will the god make hard for thee; for methinks

---

[1] " ψυχῇ χρησομένους Θηβαίου Τειρεσίαο
μάντηος ἀλαοῦ, τοῦ τε φρένες ἔμπεδοί εἰσι.' —*Od.* x. 492-498.

[2] "Ἑρμῆς δὲ ψυχὰς Κυλλήνιος ἐξεκαλεῖτο
ἀνδρῶν μνηστήρων· ἔχε δὲ ῥάβδον μετὰ χερσὶν
καλὴν χρυσείην, τῇ τ' ἀνδρῶν ὄμματα θέλγει."—*Od.* xxiv. 1-3.

The passage is, however, a disputed one.

[3] In Aristophanes, Ranæ, 1267, we have the passage—
"Ἑρμᾶν μὲν πρόγονον τίομεν γένος οἱ περὶ λίμναν,
which the Scholiast says is from the *Psychagogoi* of Æschylus.

thou shalt not pass unheeded by the Shaker of the Earth, who hath laid up wrath in his heart against thee, for rage at the blinding of his dear son. Yet even so, through many troubles, ye may come home, if thou wilt restrain thy spirit and the spirit of thy men so soon as thou shalt bring thy well-builded ship nigh to the isle Thrinacia, fleeing the sea of violet blue when ye find the herds of Helios grazing, and his brave flocks,—of Helios, who overseeth all, and overheareth all things. If thou doest these no hurt, being heedful of thy return, so may ye yet reach Ithaca, albeit in evil case. But if thou hurtest them I foreshow ruin for thy ship and for thy men; and even though thou shalt thyself escape, late shalt thou return in evil plight, with the loss of all thy company, on board the ship of strangers; and thou shalt find sorrows in thy house, even proud men that devour thy living, while they woo thy godlike wife and offer the gifts of wooing. Yet I tell thee on thy coming thou shalt avenge their violence."[1]

So far the prediction of Teiresias is verified by the issue which Homer himself narrates; the kine are stolen, the comrades of Odysseus perish to a man, the hero himself returns to his home on board the Phæakian ship; he finds in the "little isle" confusion and violence; he executes vengeance,—but before the vision of Teiresias a further future stretches of which in its accomplishment Homer says nothing.

[1] *Od.* xi. 100-116. Just such a prophecy is made to the Indian hero of the Red Swan. He too fares to the lower world, and, while he is wondering at the strange regions of light and darkness, a buffalo spirit asks him (as Anticleia asks Odysseus) how he, a living man, has dared to face the dead. The spirit further warns him that his wife is beset by evil wooers, and bids him go to her rescue. He returns to the upper world, sets his magic arrows to his bow, and lays the evil wooers at the feet of this faithful Penelope.—See H. R. Schoolcraft, *Algic Researches*, ii. 33.

"But when thou hast slain the wooers in thy halls, whether by guile, or openly with the edge of the sword, thereafter go thy way, taking with thee a shapen oar, till thou shalt come to such men as know not the sea, neither eat meat savoured with salt; yea, nor have they knowledge of ships, of vermilion cheek, nor shapen oars which serve for wings to ships."

This motive, Odysseus bearing on his shoulder the "shapen oar," we find engraven on a gem figured in Plate 30*a*. The hero wears his pilos; on the left shoulder he rests the oar, in the right hand he holds a torch; he seems to be stepping out cautiously into the darkness. The exact significance of the double attributes it is hard to determine. There may be some confusion between Odysseus descending into the darkness of the lower world and Odysseus starting on the predicted journey; or the torch may have some connection with the mysteries into which it was supposed Odysseus was initiated at Samothrace. The motive of the shapen oar is clear enough. The execution of the engraving is unusually fine.

A second gem leads us a step further in the prophecy. "And I will give thee," Teiresias continues, "a most manifest token, which cannot escape thee. In the day when another wayfarer shall meet thee and say that thou hast a winnowing-fan on thy stout shoulder, even then make fast thy shapen oar in the earth, and do goodly sacrifice to the Lord Poseidon, even with a ram and a bull and a boar, the mate of swine; and depart for home and offer holy hecatombs to the deathless gods that keep the wide heaven, to each in order due."

The witless wayfarer who "knew not of the sea" must

indeed some time have met Odysseus, for, in the design on an onyx figured in Plate 30*b*, the oar has been planted, and Odysseus stands firmly beside it. The incident seems a slight one, but this planting of the oar is the goal of the hero's long-protracted toil; and the "shapen oar" might well become the recognised symbol of endurance to the end, and as such very meet to be graven on the signet-ring worn by a faithful hand.

The genuineness of this later portion of the prophecy of Teiresias is well known to be open to doubt. It may have been interpolated to suit certain sequels to the Odyssey story composed by later poets.[1] Our gems offer no solution of the question. We have seen frequently that art borrowed its inspiration from sources other than the Homeric poem; and designs of the Græco-Roman period, such as those before us, might be derived from literature even later than the *Telegonia*. (Together with these two gems, though the moments they depict come earlier in the story, we group two other very fine gems of similar style,—Odysseus with the black ram, Plate 30*d*, and Odysseus with his foot on the slain sheep's head, Plate 30*c*.) But the seer has words of yet more mysterious and fateful import still unspoken: let us hear him to the end.

"And from the sea shall thine own death come,—the gentlest death that may be, which shall end thee foredone with smooth old age, and the folk shall dwell happily

---

[1] A grammarian says of the passage, "Nonnisi ea potuerit ætate exoriri qua cum fabula illa de Telegono conformata esset hanc rhapsodia studerent cum illa de Ulixes erroribus conjungere."

The *Telegonia* probably dates about B.C. 560; but possibly its author pirated from an earlier poem, the *Thesprotis*, composed centuries before by the mythic Musæus.

a

b

c

d

Pl. 30.

around thee. This that I say is sooth." Homer, at the close of his poem, leaves his hero resting at peace, content at last within his "little isle;" but poets of later days, brooding perhaps on these very words, "from the sea (ἐξ ἁλὸς) shall thine own death come," have fashioned for the great-hearted hero new perils and fresh voyaging through unknown seas. They fancied that the "man of many shifts" must weary of the simple, tranquil home-life by the "still hearth" among the "barren crags," and know

> "How dull it is to pause, to make an end,
> To rust unburnished, not to shine in use;"

till his longing grew to purpose, and within him and about him he felt the stirring of the sea, and he cried at last—

> "Come, my friends,
> 'Tis not too late to seek a newer world.
> Push off, and, sitting well in order, smite
> The sounding furrows; for my purpose holds
> To sail beyond the sunset, and the baths
> Of all the western stars, until I die."

Of such a second voyage and its dread end, Odysseus told to Dante, from his place of burning torment,—how he and his "small company" fared by the Pillars of Hercules, and saw ahead a vision of a mighty mountain, and their joy was turned to weeping;

> "For out of the new land a whirlwind rose,
> And smote upon the forepart of the ship;"

and so they perished by a fell sea doom.

We may well suppose that about this mysterious death of Odysseus, the ancients, as well as the moderns, wove their traditions. The Cyclic poets rumour that he perished by the spear of Telegonus, son of Circe. This spear was tipped by the poison of a fish, and so the hero's death came to him *from the sea*. If we turn to Plate 31, we shall see a quaint variation of this tradition.[1]

A boat is nearing the shore; in it are two sailors; the foremost one is fixing his anchor—the goal of the voyage is evidently reached; the second sailor still works his oar. Above his head flies a sort of heron holding in his mouth a ray-fish, the poisonous trygon (τρύγων), which still endangers the Mediterranean waters. The heron is about to let fall his prey; its long stinging tail hangs directly over the rower's head. This rower is presumably Odysseus. The beautiful lady seated on the shore may be the patient Penelope, or she may be merely a coast nymph. All three figures are very youthful—too youthful to accord well with the explanation. We might be in doubt as to the situation intended, but the sceptic Sextus Empiricus (not usually a writer fruitful in suggestion) comes to our aid. He says, in his grumbling way, how can he attach importance to historical tradition when "one man says, for example, that Odysseus died by the hand of his son Telegonos, another that he breathed his last owing to a sea-gull which let fall on his head the sting of a ray-fish."[2] Such a death assuredly is about to befall the rower in our vase-

[1] The design in Plate 31 is taken from the Vasi Fittili of Inghirami. Since it was drawn it was long supposed that the original vase had perished, but it has been rediscovered at the Porcinari House, Naples. The following inscriptions have been made out:—Above the woman's head ΠΟΝΤΙΑ, which would accord with the supposition that she is a sea or coast nymph; above the head of the foremost sailor ΔΑΙΜΟΣ, meaning unknown; above the head of the rower ΚΑΜ-ΡΙΣ. Odysseus was, we know, called by his mother κάμμορε φωτῶν, and the two forms *may* have some connection.

[2] "τινὸς μὲν λέγοντος ὅτι 'Οδυσσεὺς ὑπὸ Τηλεγόνου παιδὸς κατὰ ἄγνοιαν ἀνήρηται τινὸς δὲ ὅτι λάρου κέντρον θαλασσίας τρυγόνος ἀφέντος αὐτοῦ τῇ κεφαλῇ διεφώνησεν."—SEXT. EMPIR., *Adv. Gramm.*, 273.

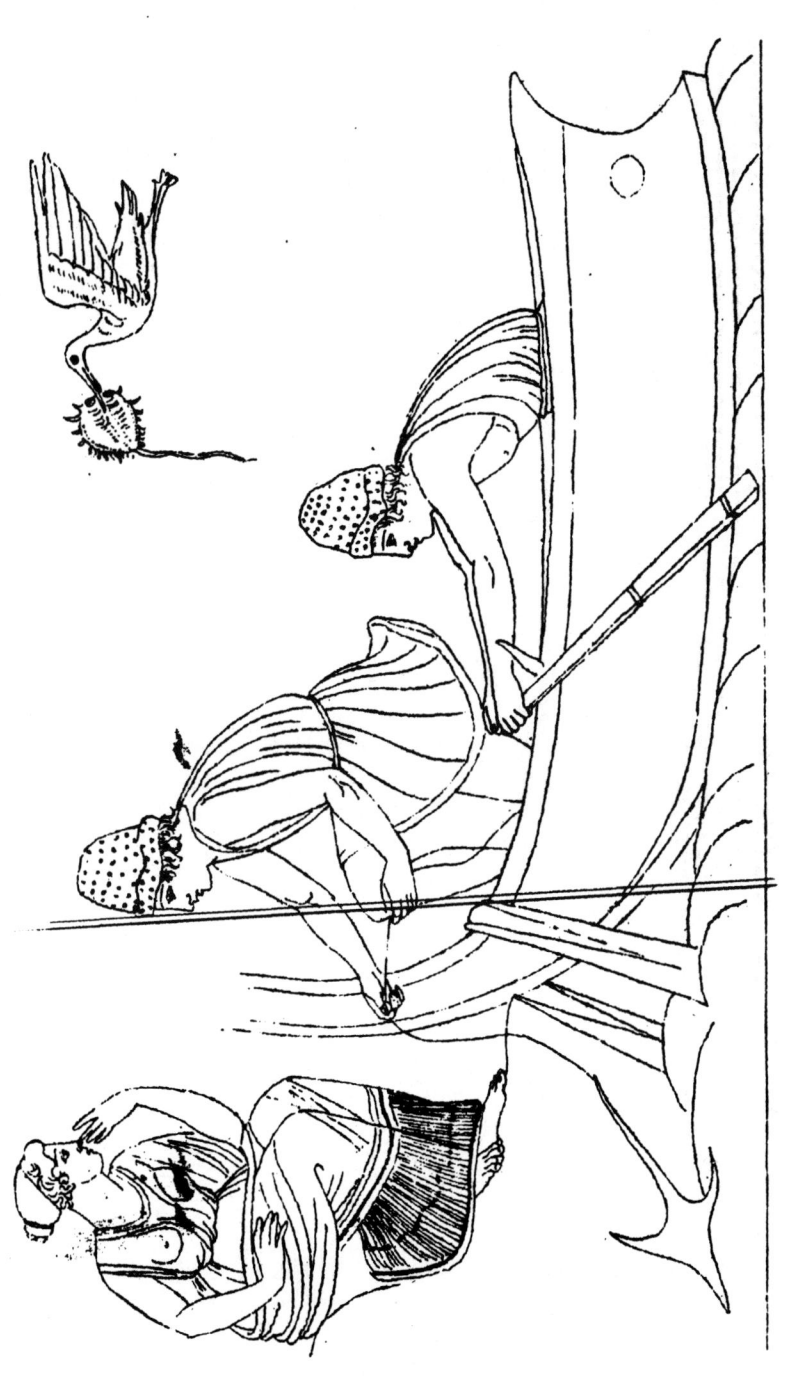

painting, whether he be Odysseus or not. A similar fate, though in less picturesque form, was, we know, prophesied for Odysseus by the seer Teiresias in the *Psychagogoi* of Æschylus.[1] It is thought that the issue *foretold* in the *Psychagogoi* may have been *accomplished* in a second or third drama of the same trilogy, bearing possibly the title of Odysseus the Sting-Pierced (ἀκανθοπλήξ). Such a drama we know to have been written by Sophokles, but no notice of its contents has been preserved us.

These literary memorials of a later tradition are too curious, and our vase-painting too beautiful, to have been passed over in silence; but already the oracles of the "prince Teiresias" have detained us too long, and we must suffer the spirit of the seer to go back within the house of Hades, for a mighty throng presses behind him.

Next in order draws near the shade of Anticleia, the daughter of Autolycus the great-hearted. Of this pathetic meeting between Odysseus and the soul of his mother, art has left us no certain monument. It was the subject of a noted decorative design in the temple of Apollo at Cyzicus, but the only record left us of it is an epigram in the Anthology.[2]

---

[1] Scholiast on Odyss. xi. 134, says that Æschylus in his *Psychagogoi* describes how the heron (Ἐρωδιός) swallowed the poisonous fish itself, and hence—

"ἐκ τοῦδ' ἄκανθα ποντίου βοσκήματος
σήψει παλαιὸν δέρμα καὶ τριχορροές,"

the bird is described just as it appears in our vase-painting, *i.e.*, "ὑψόθι ποτώμενος."

[2] "Μᾶτερ Ὀδυσσῆος πινυτόφρονος Ἀντίκλεια
ζῶσα μὲν εἰς Ἰθάκην οὐκ ὑπέδεξο πάϊν
ἀλλά σε νῦν Ἀχέροντος ἐπὶ ῥηγμῖσι γεγῶσαν
θαμβεῖ ἀνὰ γλυκερὰν ματέρα δερκόμενος."
Anth. Palat. iii. 8.

In our first picture (the wall-painting in Autotype VI.) we left the shades of the mighty women of the past thronging the reedy background. To them we must return, for while Anticleia has told her sad story, they wait to have speech of Odysseus.

"And lo, the women came up; for the high goddess Persephone sent them forth, all they that had been the wives and daughters of mighty men. And they gathered and pressed about the black blood, and I took counsel how I might question them each one. And this was the counsel that showed best in my sight. I drew my long hanger from my stalwart thigh, and suffered them not all at one time to drink of the dark blood."[1]

We note, almost with regret, how, again and again, this ritual point, the drinking of the dark blood, is emphasised. This Nekyia, this "Book of the Dead," is, we are obliged to own, if not "steeped" yet at least tinged "with the Animism of barbarous peoples."[2] In the mythologies, alike of nations the most barbarous as well as the most cultured, the soul is conceived of as a sort of shadowy material shape, to be revivified by the same material essence as the body itself, by that blood which is the life. For this warm draught of life the ghosts are greedy.

Only three of the fourteen famous women who declared to Odysseus their lineage can be identified in our landscape. Phædra (ΦΑΙΔΡΑ) is clearly inscribed; Homer only mentions her in passing:[3] "and I saw Phædra." Later we shall meet her again on the walls of the Lesche at Delphi, with the symbol of her destruction in her hands. Ariadne (ΑΡΙΑΔΝΕ) is also plainly inscribed, and Homer tells her

[1] *Od.* xi.   [2] See *Hellenica*, page 437.   [3] *Od.* xi. 321.

tale—"fair Ariadne, the daughter of wizard Minos, whom Theseus on a time was bearing from Crete to the slope of sacred Athens. Yet had he no joy of her; for Artemis slew her ere that, in sea-girt Dia, by reason of the witness of Dionysos."[1] Ariadne, too, will meet us in the Lesche with her sister, sadder even than herself.

Our third inscribed fair woman is Leda (EΔA). The L of the inscription is lost; the remaining letters are clear. She, Homer tells us,[2] was "the famous bedfellow of Tyndareus, who bare to Tyndareus two sons hardy of heart,—Castor, tamer of steeds, and Polydeuces the boxer."

In the reedy background we have to fancy the ghosts of a throng of other women, "wives and daughters of heroes," Tyro, Antiope, Alcmene, Epicaste, Chloris, Iphimedeia, Prokris, Mæra, Clymene, Eriphyle. Of these we shall meet again all but Tyro, Alcmene, and Epicaste, when we come to consider the great picture of Polygnotus.

After "holy Persephone had scattered this way and that the spirits of the women folk,"[3] the heroes came up to have speech. Agamemnon and Achilles, and Patroclus and Archilochus; only the soul of Aias stood apart, sullen and vengeful.[4] These heroes, too, we shall later behold in the Delphian Lesche; for the present we must turn to our second Hades landscape from the Esquiline series, and note the scenes that are there depicted. The ghosts now in view, we observe, no longer throng to approach Odysseus; he seems to have sight into the innermost depths of hell.[5]

[1] *Od.* xi. 321.   [2] *Od.* xi. 298.   [3] *Od.* xi. 385, 386.   [4] *Od.* xi. 544.

[5] This incongruity has led to the supposition that the whole passage is interpolated to suit later conventional representations of Hades. Lauer, arguing from the Theban origin of Teiresias and many of the heroines, supposes that the whole νεκυία is of Bœotian authorship. See Lauer, *Literarischer Nachlass.*

The landscape figured in Autotype VII. is unhappily much mutilated. The design seems to have been rudely interrupted. Possibly some barbarian hand may have broken through the picture to make a door or window. It was clearly not intended for a half picture. To the left we see a large overhanging rock; beneath it a narrow stream, on the opposite side of which rises hilly ground. Here lies full length an outstretched figure—we do not need the inscription (ΤΙΤΥΟΣ) to tell us his name. His enormous size is somewhat diminished for artistic purposes by the foreshortening his position necessitates. Two vultures, one of which is very indistinct, tear at his liver; with his left hand he seems to try without success to keep them at bay. The Homeric description has been closely followed. "And I saw Tityos, son of renowned Earth, lying on a levelled ground, and he covered nine roods as he lay; and vultures twain beset him, one on either side, and gnawed at his liver, piercing even to the caul; but he drove them not away with his hands. For he had dealt violently with Leto, the famous bedfellow of Zeus, as she went up to Pytho through the fair lawns of Panopeus."[1] Worn out at last with punishment for this awful sacrilege, we shall see him in the Lesche of that very shrine of Pytho, to which Leto was going.

Equally clear is the inscription and the attitude of Sisyphus (ΣΙΣΥΦΟΣ), whom Odysseus saw, "in strong torment, grasping a monstrous stone with both his hands. He was pressing thereat with hands and feet, and trying to roll the stone towards the brow of the hill. But oft as he was about to hurl it over the top the weight would

[1] *Od.* xi. 576.

VII

drive him back, so once again to the plain rolled the stone—the pitiless thing. And he once more kept heaving and straining, and the sweat the while was pouring down his limbs, and the dust rose upwards from his head."[1] Sisyphus, too, is numbered, as we shall see, among the fruitless labourers in the hall at Delphi, whose hell is their bootless toil.

So far all is clear, but above Sisyphus there stands in our picture a naked youth of threatening aspect. No inscription helps us. In connection with Sisyphus and Tityos Homer mentions only Tantalus, Herakles, Minos, Orion. Tantalus is impossible; probably he occupied in part the lost right-hand part of the picture. Herakles would naturally have held the three-headed Cerberus; Minos would have been seated on his throne. Only Orion is left; and on the whole our figure tallies with Homer's description: "I marked the mighty Orion driving the wild beasts together over the mead of asphodel, the very beasts that himself had slain on the lonely hills, with a strong mace all of bronze in his hands, that is ever unbroken."[2] The gesture of the figure is certainly that of a man driving on something ahead of him. The giant stature is seen by the fact that his size is the same as that of the women in the foreground, though some allowance must be made for inadequate knowledge of perspective. The object he holds in his hand is indistinct, but it might be intended for the "strong mace, all of bronze."

Of the scene presented in the foreground Homer tells us nothing; but the intent is obvious. Round a huge vessel, half buried in the ground, are grouped four female

[1] *Od.* xi. 593. [2] *Od.* xi. 572.

figures. Their arms are bare; they wear head-dresses; the centre figure has emptied her jug; two others are in the act of pouring out their water; the fourth seems to turn away to refill her vessel; a fifth has gone to the river to replenish her jar, and sits down a while, sorrowful and exhausted. The inscription is effaced but for three letters, ΑΙΔ; the remainder are obviously thus supplied:— ΔΑΝ]ΑΙΔ[ΕΣ (Danaides). We shall see in the picture of Polygnotus, not indeed these actual Danaides, but a group analogous to them,—a family of the Uninitiated, who for ever carry water in vain in leaking jars. I believe that our landscape-painter had come to regard some such figures as these as a sort of necessary conventional symbol of Hades; but, desirous of making his presentation Epic rather than Orphic, he gave to his fruitless toilers the title of Danaides.

We have learnt to know how the Hades of Homer appeared to the fancy of the Augustan wall-painter. Though his work is somewhat marred by time, enough remains to allow of a clear and vivid conception. The painter's name is lost, but his pictures remain,—a lasting treasure. Another artist[1] had already depicted on walls of world-wide fame this Hades scene. The name of Polygnotus is still honoured among men; but no fragment of this, his greatest work, has survived the wreck of time. Some four hundred years before the Greek painter began to decorate

[1] A famous Νεκυία was also painted by a *third* artist, the celebrated Nikias, more than a century later than Polygnotus, but no description remains of it; we only know that he refused to sell it to Attalus for sixty talents, and presented it to his native city of Athens. See Plut. xi. 2; Pliny, *N.H.* xxxv. 132; and *Anthol.* ix. 792.

for a wealthy Roman his house on the Esquiline Hill, Polygnotus, by command of the Cnidians, adorned the walls of their Lesche at Delphi with a design, depicting on the right hand the taking of Troy, on the left the descent of Odysseus into Hades. Though his work has wholly perished, there remains for us a detailed description. Seven whole chapters are devoted by Pausanias to his account of the wall-paintings of the Lesche, and however uncritical, almost incoherent, we may consider his loose narrative, to it we must turn as our main source for information.

The task of reconstructing these Lesche pictures from the meagre material of these travellers' notes has fascinated archæologists from all times. The subject has a literature to itself,—a literature of absorbing interest, and sometimes amazing ingenuity. The problem to be solved is, briefly, What and in what manner did Polygnotus paint in the hall at Delphi? In what sequence were his subjects placed, and with what degree of artistic perfection did he render them? The materials for its solution are the narrative of Pausanias, the literary sources (whether written or verbally traditional) to which Polygnotus resorted for his mythology, our knowledge generally of his style, and the treatment of analogous subjects by other artists. Of these topics time and space alike forbid the exhaustive treatment. We must be content if, with Pausanias at hand, and the restoration of the modern artist before our eyes, we may stand in spirit for a while in the Delphian Lesche, and see clearly at least, if not completely, some shadow of the ghosts that throng the kingdoms of Persephone. Let us turn to Plate 32.

To the left of the picture is seen a river, which Pausanias says is evidently Acheron.[1] In its ghastly waters dank reeds are growing, and shadowy fishes can be dimly seen. The foreground of our Esquiline landscape picture, we have seen, was thickly overgrown with rushes, no doubt suggested by the swamps of Avernus; this is perhaps the only point in which the two pictures clearly resemble each other. On the river is a boat, and a ferryman sitting to his oars, the ancient Charon. This Charon,[2] unknown to Homer, Pausanias thinks was borrowed by Polygnotus from the Minyas,[3] where the ferryman is introduced refusing to admit to his boat Theseus and Pirithoös. The shades whom Charon ferries across are too dim for their relationship[4] to be clearly made out; two only Pausanias recognises, the maiden Cleobeia and the youth Tellis. The maiden carries on her knee the sacred cista; she it was who first brought to her island home of Thasos (the painter's birthplace) the mysteries of Demeter. We shall never know what was the tale of love and sacrifice and early death which brought these two unwed to Charon's boat; but they cross together, and bear with them the symbol of sacred joy. Below, in contrast perhaps to this scene of holy bliss, we see an impious son strangled in Hades by an avenging father, and a

[1] "ὕδωρ εἶναι ποταμὸς ἔοικε, δῆλα ὡς ὁ Ἀχέρων, καὶ κάλαμοί τε ἐν αὐτῷ πεφυκότες, καὶ ἀμυδρὰ οὕτω δή τι τὰ εἴδη τῶν ἰχθύων σκιὰς μᾶλλον ἢ ἰχθῦς εἰκάσεις· καὶ ναῦς ἐστιν ἐν τῷ ποταμῷ καὶ ὁ πορθμεὺς ἐπὶ ταῖς κώπαις."—PAUS. x. 28.

[2] Charon still lives on in modern Greece as Charos or Charontas. But he is now no longer a mere ferryman, rather he is a terrible impersonation of Hades itself. He rides a coal-black horse, his eyes gleam fire, and, Erlkönig fashion, he drags off children from their struggling parents.

[3] "ἐπηκολούθησε δὲ ὁ Πολύγνωτος ἐμοὶ δοκεῖν ποιήσει Μινυάδι."—PAUS. x. 28.

[4] "οἱ δὲ ἐπιβεβηκότες τῆς νεὼς οὐκ ἐπιφανεῖς εἰς ἅπαν εἰσὶν οἷς προσήκουσι." This vague sentence leaves quite undetermined the number of persons in the boat. Possibly there were only Tellis and Cleobeia.

Pl 32.

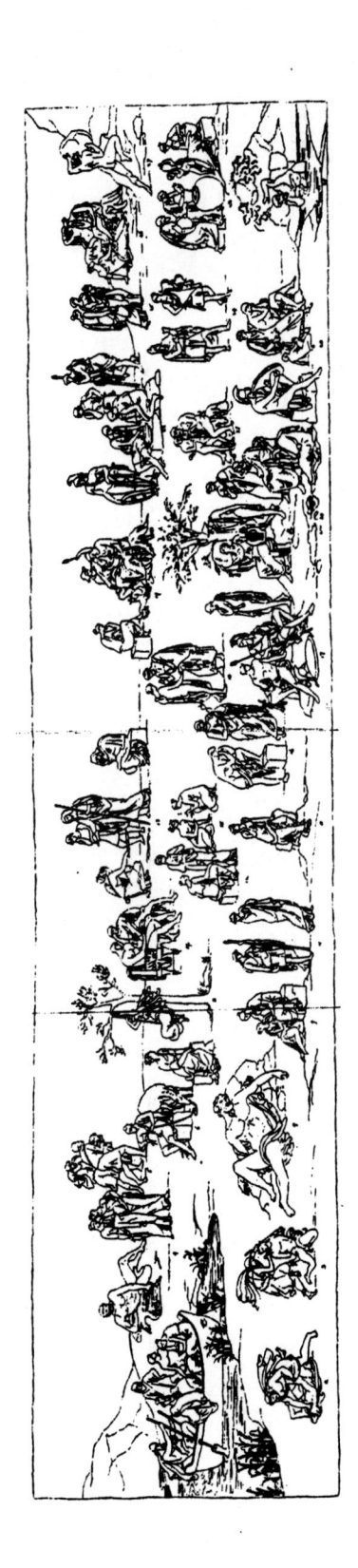

man tortured for sacrilege. Above the criminals, and above the boat of Charon, watches a grim and terrible fiend, of whom no author known to Pausanias makes mention, a Delphic Hades-demon, Eurynomus,[1] of "blue-black colour, like flesh-eating flies." He lies upon a vulture's skin, and shows his savage teeth.

So far the figures presented by Polygnotus are foreign to the Odyssey story; but next to the fiend Eurynomus are standing two matrons, Auge, the goodliest of the wives of Herakles, and Iphimedeia, who told to Odysseus the story of her mighty sons, how they sought to "pile a pathway" to the skies, but the son of Leto slew them.[2] Above the matrons are two figures of special interest for us, Perimedes and Eurylochus. They are represented carrying the victims, black rams. Apparently they were separated from Odysseus by some considerable interval. After them is a man seated, inscribed Ocnus; his quaint companion relieves by a touch of humour the gloom of Hades. Ocnus[3] is twisting a rope; near him stands a she-ass, who eats the rope as fast as he twists. Ocnus it seems was in the upper

---

[1] Pausanias distinctly states that no such demon was described either in the Minyas or the Nostoi; and for the name and nature of Eurynomus he relies on the guides; probably the fiend embodied some local conception—

"δαίμονα εἶναι τῶν ἐν Ἅιδου φασὶν οἱ Δελφῶν ἐξηγηταὶ τὸν Εὐρύνομον, καὶ ὡς τὰς σάρκας περιεσθίει τῶν νεκρῶν, μόνα σφίσιν ἀπολείπων τὰ ὀστᾶ."—PAUS. x. 28.

And again—

"ἡ δὲ Ὁμήρου ποίησις ἡ ἐς Ὀδυσσέα καὶ ἡ Μινυάς τε καλουμένη καὶ οἱ Νόστοι ἴσασιν οὐδένα Εὐρύνομον."—PAUS. x. 28.

[2] Od. xi. 315-320:—

"Ὄσσαν ἐπ' Ὀλύμπῳ μέμασαν θέμεν αὐτὰρ ἐπ' Ὄσσῃ
Πήλιον εἰνοσίφυλλον, ἵν' οὐρανὸς ἀμβατὸς εἴη."

[3] An Ocnus occurred in some play by Kratinus. See Meinecke, Fr. Com. ii. 203:—

"Ἀρίσταρχος δὲ διὰ τὸ Κρατῖνον ὑπόθεσθαι ἐν Ἅιδου σχοινίον πλέκοντα, ὄνον δὲ τὸ πλεκόμενον ἀπεσθίοντα."

world an industrious man, with an extravagant wife; perhaps he was a miser, else why in Hades is this conjugal discipline protracted? The feeling here is certainly rather Hesiodic than Homeric. Near to this humorous pair lies a shadowy shape, more terrible because so dim, Tityos, tortured no longer, but worn out through ceaseless punishment.[1] In our landscape-painting we have seen the vultures tear him; we feel how much grander is this conception of the exhausted ghost. Above this figure, close to the thrifty Ocnus and his mate, we meet another familiar pair. Ariadne sits upon a rock, and looks towards her sister Phædra. Phædra holds in both her hands a rope, and from it her body is suspended. The description of Pausanias is so vague, it is hard to say how the unhappy Phædra hung; the traveller only adds that, "though the attitude was pleasing and becoming, it indicated the manner of her death.[2]

Beneath these luckless sisters must have been depicted a charming group—somewhat analogous, perhaps, to the so-called Herse and Pandrosos of the Parthenon—lovely Chloris reclining against the knees of her dear friend Thyia, for

[1] "γέγραπται δὲ καὶ Τιτυὸς οὐ κολαζόμενος ἔτι ἀλλὰ ὑπὸ τοῦ συνεχοῦς τῆς τιμωρίας ἐς ἅπαν ἐξανηλωμένος ἀμυδρὸν καὶ οὐδὲ ὁλόκληρον εἴδωλον."—PAUS. x.

[2] "(Ἀριάδνη) κάθηται μὲν ἐπὶ πέτρας ὁρᾷ δὲ ἐς τὴν ἀδελφὴν Φαίδραν τό τε ἄλλο αἰωρουμένην σῶμα ἐν σειρᾷ καὶ ταῖς χερσὶν ἀμφοτέρωθεν τῆς σειρᾶς ἐχομένην. Παρεῖχε δὲ τὸ σχῆμα καίπερ ἐς τὸ εὐπρεπέστερον πεποιημένον συμβάλλεσθαι τὰ ἐς τῆς Φαίδρας τὴν τελευτήν."

The manner depicted by the modern artist is no fanciful conceit, but would be quite consonant with Greek tradition. It appears that at the festival of the Attic Aiora the women of Athens were wont to swing themselves, in memory of an Attic heroine, Erigone, who died the death of Phædra. They sang during this to us somewhat ghastly pastime a song by Theodorus of Colophon. Vase pictures with female figures swinging occur not unfrequently; they may have some reference to this ceremony.

between these two, the traveller tells us, great love subsisted. Of Chloris Homer sang that she was bride of Neleus and bare glorious children to her lord, among them "stately Pero, the wonder of all men."[1] Near to them, standing alone, is jealous Prokris, whom unwittingly her husband slew, and after her comes Clymene, also the bride of Kephalos. Not far away is Theban Megara seated sadly alone; her Herakles put away because her children perished by the hand of the gods. Above the heads of these women the daughter of Salmoneus is seated on a stone, and near her stands "hateful Eriphyle, who took fine gold for the price of her dear lord's life."[2] She feels with her finger tips for her neck through the folds of her garment; perchance the necklet still burns there. Still higher in the picture, and possibly in a central position, we see the group already so familiar. Odysseus crouches on his knees[3] and holds a sword over the ditch. The prophet Teiresias approaches, and after Teiresias is figured Anticleia seated, waiting, on a stone. Near to Odysseus is Elpenor, not, as we saw him in our landscape, holding aloof. The attitude of Odysseus (ὀκλάζοντα ἐπὶ τοῖς ποσίν) is markedly different from that we have seen in the vase-painting. Some analogy is observable between this description of Pausanias and the ungainly posture in the Esquiline wall-picture. Elpenor's dress is carefully noted; he wears a gar-

[1] "τοῖσι δ' ἐπ' ἰφθίμην Πηρὼ τέκε θαῦμα βροτοῖσι."—*Od.* xi 287.

[2] "στυγερήν τ' Ἐριφύλην
ἣ χρυσὸν φίλου ἀνδρὸς ἐδέξατο τιμήεντα."—*Od.* xi. 326, 327.

[3] "ὑπὲρ δὲ τὴν Ἐριφύλην ἔγραψεν Ἐλπήνορά τε καὶ Ὀδυσσέα ὀκλάζοντα ἐπὶ τοῖς ποσὶν ἔχοντα ὑπὲρ τοῦ βόθρου τὸ ξίφος, καὶ ὁ μάντις Τειρεσίας πρόεισιν ἐπὶ τὸν βόθρον· μετὰ δὲ τὸν Τειρεσίαν ἐπὶ πέτρας ἡ Ὀδυσσέως μήτηρ Ἀντίκλεια ἐστιν."—Paus. x. 28.

ment made of rushes after the manner of sailors.[1] Beneath Odysseus are seated the pair whom Homer tells us the hero was "fain to see, Theseus and Peirithoos, renowned children of the gods."[2] They are represented seated on a throne together—in their death they were not divided. Theseus holds in his hands both his own sword and that of Peirithoos. Pausanias fancies that Peirithoos looks at the swords with angry eyes, indignant that they may not serve him for bold deeds.

After this pair of friends come the two daughters of Pandareus. So goodly was their nurture we cannot forbear to tell of it as Penelope[3] told in her prayer to Artemis. "Their father and their mother the gods had slain, and the maidens were left orphans in the halls, and fair Aphrodite cherished them with curds and sweet honey and delicious wine. And Here gave them beauty and wisdom beyond the lot of women, and holy Artemis dowered them with stature, and Athene taught them skill in all famous handiwork." But alas! rude fate cut short this gentle tendance. "Now,

---

[1] "ἀμπέχεται φορμὸν ἀντὶ ἐσθῆτος σύνηθες τοῖς ναύταις φόρημα"—the wonted garment, too, of fishermen, according to Theokritus.—*Id.* xxi. 13.

[2] "καὶ νύ κ' ἔτι προτέρους ἴδον ἀνέρας οὓς ἔθελόν περ·
Θησέα Πειρίθοόν τε, θεῶν ἐρικυδέα τέκνα."—*Od.* xi. 631.

[3] "τῆσι τοκῆας μὲν φθῖσαν θεοί, αἱ δ' ἐλίποντο
ὀρφαναὶ ἐν μεγάροισι κόμισσε δὲ δῖ' Ἀφροδίτη
τυρῷ καὶ μέλιτι γλυκερῷ καὶ ἡδέϊ οἴνῳ
Ἥρη δ' αὐτῇσιν περὶ πασέων δῶκε γυναικῶν
εἶδος καὶ πινυτὴν μῆκος δ' ἔπορ' Ἄρτεμις ἁγνὴ
ἔργα δ' Ἀθηναίη δέδαε κλυτὰ ἐργάζεσθαι.
Εὖτ' Ἀφροδίτη δῖα προσέστιχε μακρὸν Ὄλυμπον
κούρῃς αἰτήσουσα τέλος θαλεροῖο γάμοιο
ἐς Δία τερπικέραυνον. . . . .
τόφρα δὲ τὰς κούρας Ἅρπυιαι ἀνηρείψαντο
καὶ ῥ' ἔδοσαν στυγερῇσιν Ἐρινύσιν ἀμφιπολεύειν."

Od. xx. 67.

while fair Aphrodite was wending to high Olympus to pray that a glad marriage might be accomplished for the maidens, and to Zeus she went whose joy is in the thunder . . , in the meanwhile the spirits of the storm snatched away these maidens, and gave them to be handmaids to the hateful Erinnyes." In Hades they are crowned by Polygnotus with flowers, and, because unwed, play, girl fashion, with the astragaloi,[1] symbols perhaps of Fate.

After the two daughters of Pandareus comes a series of Trojan heroes. Antilochus, with one foot on a stone,—noble Antilochus, whom Odysseus spake with in Hades. After him the soul of Agamemnon, son of Atreus, still the king of men, for he leans with his left arm on a sceptre, and holds in both hands a wand. We know the sad tale he had to tell to Odysseus, and the embittered counsel that, all unneeded, he proffered. Three other mighty Trojan heroes are nigh at hand; Achilles and Protesilaus, seated, gaze at each other; near them stands Patroklus. Above, two friends, young Phocus and aged Iascus; from the finger of Phocus Iascus draws a ring—pledge of fidelity.

Above them, again, Mæra is seated alone on a stone; her too Odysseus saw. She was a heroine of the Nostoi, and died a virgin. After Mæra, Actæon the huntsman, with his mother; she holds a fawn in her hand; near them is a hound to show the manner of the youth's death.

Beneath these figures, in the lower part of the picture, is a group at which we well may gaze with earnest eyes. Upon a hillock, leaning against a sacred tree, is seated the

---

[1] Some echo, perhaps, of the motive of this lovely group we may have in the terracotta-maidens playing with astragaloi, now in the British Museum. Guide to 2d Vase Room, Part II., page 96.

minstrel Orpheus, clad in simple Greek dress. In his left hand he holds a lyre, and with his right he touches a willow branch.[1] Exactly what mystic significance Polygnotus attached to this Orpheus figure we shall probably never know; around his name has grown "a web of hopes and emotions which no hand can disentangle now."[2] Odysseus tells us nothing of the prophet bard; in his days mysticism had not cast over Hellas that cloud which, at the first softly transparent, was soon to deepen into darkness. This lute of Orpheus, sounding in Hades, rouses us to note how far, from key to key, the music of faith had wandered since Homer's simple song. Orpheus, in a later Hades picture, we shall meet again; at present beside him are listening Promedon, leaning also on the willow, Schedios, and hoary Pelias seated on a throne. Schedios is crowned with reeds and holds a dagger. Near to Pelias sits sightless Thamyris, his shattered lyre beside him; he himself, Pausanias notes, looks humbled and dejected. All these are shaded by the sacred grove of Persephone.[3] Above them is Marsyas sitting on the stone; he teaches to the boy Olympus his art of piping. Still further above come a group of Trojans, enemies of Odysseus, whom Polygnotus (Pausanias thinks) has purposely collected in one place. Palamedes and Thersites play with the dice which Palamedes[4] on earth invented. Between this group and

[1] "ἀποβλέψαντι δὲ αὖθις ἐς τὰ κάτω τῆς γραφῆς ἔστιν ἐφεξῆς μετὰ τὸν Πάτροκλον οἷα ἐπὶ λόφου τινὸς Ὀρφεὺς καθεζόμενος, ἐφάπτεται δὲ καὶ τῇ ἀριστερᾷ κιθάρας, τῇ δὲ ἑτέρᾳ χειρὶ ἰτέας κλῶνές εἰσιν ὧν ψαύει, προσανακέκλιται δὲ τῷ δένδρῳ."

[2] See Mr. F. W. H. Myers' Greek Oracles—*Hellenica*, p. 459.

[3] "ἔνθ' ἀκτή τε λάχεια καὶ ἄλσεα Περσεφονείης
μακραί τ' αἴγειροι καὶ ἰτέαι ὠλεσίκαρποι."—*Od.* x. 510, 511.

[4] Palamedes, unknown to Homer, a prominent hero in the Cyclic poems and a not infrequent figure in vase-paintings.

Actæon stands Salaminian Aias, the only shade (we remember) who remained sullenly apart,[1] and refused to have speech of Odysseus, even in Hades remembering his enmity. Watching the dice players stands the other Aias, the son of Oileus, whom Odysseus, for his daring to Cassandra, desired to stone to death. Above this Aias stands Meleager, of whom Homer[2] tells us that he died at the hand of the Erinnys through the curse of Althæa. In the lowest part of the picture sits Hector, his hands about his knee, in deep depression; next to him Memnon, with one hand on the shoulder of Sarpedon. Memnon wears a robe decorated with painted birds. Near Memnon is a naked Æthiopian boy. This beautiful hero we shall meet again depicted in the wall decoration of an Etruscan tomb. Above Memnon and Sarpedon is Paris, yet a beardless youth; he seems to clap his hands in token that he calls Penthesilea, but she turns away, scorning him. She is attired like a virgin huntress, with Scythian bow and leopard skin.

Above these two are the figures of two women, one young, one old They carry water in jars with holes. Instinctively we think of the Danaides, but Pausanias tells us that a common inscription denotes them as two of the uninitiated, and then our thoughts turn to Sokrates,[3] and we remember how a "certain ingenious man of Italy or

---

[1] " οἴη δ' Αἴαντος ψυχὴ Τελαμωνιάδαο
νόσφιν ἀφεστήκει, κεχολωμένη εἵνεκα νίκης."—*Od.* xi. 543, 544.

[2] See *Iliad.* ix. 571:—
" κικλήσκουσ' Ἀΐδην καὶ ἐπαινὴν Περσεφόνειαν
πρόχνυ καθεζομένη, δεύοντο δὲ δάκρυσι κόλποι
παιδὶ δόμεν θάνατον· τῆς δ' ἠεροφοῖτις Ἐρινὺς
ἔκλυεν."

[3] " καὶ τοῦτ' ἄρα τις μυθολογῶν κομψὸς ἀνὴρ ἴσως Σικελός τις ἢ Ἰταλικός, παράγων τῷ ὀνόματι διὰ τὸ πιθανόν τε καὶ πιστικὸν ὠνόμασε πίθον, τοὺς δὲ

Sicily" told him a fable that the appetites of the uninitiate soul were as a leaky jar, figuring thereby its insatiate nature. Did this "ingenious man of Sicily," Empedokles perhaps, ever gaze on the picture of Polygnotus and see these women, these uninitiate souls, seek for ever in vain to draw water from the wells of salvation? If not Empedokles, at least Sokrates, the first of ethical philosophers, would surely sometime ponder this masterpiece of the greatest ethical painter.[1]

After these hapless, thirsty souls a group of three fair figures follows. Callisto, with the hide of a bear for the covering of her couch, her feet resting on the lap of the Arcadian nymph Nomia, and for the third "stately Pero," whose wooer must needs "drive off the kine" of Tyro that Iphikles held.[2]

After this group of goodly women there rises a precipice up which Sisyphus toils for ever to raise his mighty stone. Below him more water-carriers enduring fruitless labour with perforated jars; these again are the uninitiated—an old man, an old woman, a matron, and a boy, each sex and every age. Below again, and last of all, is Tantalus in torment, as

ἀνοήτους ἀμυήτους· τῶν δὲ ἀμυήτων τοῦτο τῆς ψυχῆς οὗ αἱ ἐπιθυμίαι εἰσί, τὸ ἀκόλαστον αὐτοῦ καὶ οὐ στεγανόν, ὡς τετρημένος εἴη πίθος, διὰ τὴν ἀπληστίαν ἀπεικάσας. τοὐναντίον δὴ οὗτός σοι, ὦ Καλλίκλεις, ἐνδείκνυται ὡς τῶν ἐν Ἅιδου— τὸ ἀειδὲς δὴ λέγων—οὗτοι ἀθλιώτατοι ἂν εἶεν οἱ ἀμύητοι καὶ φοροῖεν εἰς τὸν τετρημένον πίθον ὕδωρ ἑτέρῳ τοιούτῳ τετρημένῳ κοσκίνῳ."—*Plat. Gorg.* 493, A. B. See Paus. x. 31.

[1] "οὐ μὴν ἀλλ' ὅσον διαφέρει καὶ περὶ τὴν τούτων θεωρίαν, δεῖ μὴ τὰ Παύσωνος θεωρεῖν τοὺς νέους, ἀλλὰ τὰ Πολυγνώτου κἂν εἴ τις ἄλλος τῶν γραφέων ἢ τῶν ἀγαλματοποιῶν ἐστὶν ἠθικός."—*Aristot. Polit.* viii. 5, 7.

[2] "τοῖσι δ' ἐπ' ἰφθίμην Πηρὼ τέκε θαῦμα βροτοῖσι
τὴν πάντες μνώοντο περικτίται· οὐδέ τι Νηλεὺς
τῷ ἐδίδου ὃς μὴ ἕλικας βόας εὐρυμετώπους
ἐκ Φυλάκης ἐλάσειε βίης Ἰφικληείης."—*Od.* xi. 287-290.

Odysseus saw him[1] "standing in a mere, and the water came nigh unto his chin. And he stood straining as one athirst, but he might not attain to the water to drink of it. For often as that old man stooped down in his eagerness to drink, so often the water was swallowed up and it vanished away, and the black earth still showed at his feet, for some god parched it evermore. And tall trees flowering shed their fruit overhead, pears and pomegranates, and apple-trees with bright fruit, and sweet figs and olives in their bloom, whereat, when that old man reached out his hands to clutch them, the wind would toss them to the shadowy clouds." To this lingering torment, surely grievous enough, Polygnotus had added a more instant horror;[2] in his picture, above the old man hangs a mighty rock, ever ready to fall upon him. In this addition Pausanias says he clearly followed Archilochos; the painter and the poet were alike of Thasian birth.

[1] " καὶ μὴν Τάνταλον εἰσεῖδον χαλέπ' ἄλγε' ἔχοντα
ἑστεῶτ' ἐν λίμνῃ· ἡ δὲ προσέπλαζε γενείῳ·
στεῦτο δὲ διψάων, πιέειν δ'οὐχ εἶχεν ἑλέσθαι·
ὁσσάκι γὰρ κύψει' ὁ γέρων πιέειν μενεαίνων
τοσσάχ' ὕδωρ ἀπολέσκετ' ἀναβροχέν, ἀμφὶ δὲ ποσσὶ
γαῖα μέλαινα φάνεσκε, καταζήνασκε δὲ δαίμων·
δένδρεα δ'ὑψιπέτηλα κατὰ κρῆθεν χέε καρπὸν,
ὄγχναι καὶ ῥοιαὶ καὶ μηλέαι ἀγλαόκαρποι
συκέαι τε γλυκεραὶ καὶ ἐλαῖαι τηλεθόωσαι
τῶν ὁπότ' ἰθύσει' ὁ γέρων ἐπὶ χερσὶ μάσασθαι,
τὰς δ' ἄνεμος ῥίπτασκε ποτὶ νέφεα σκιόεντα."
        Od. xi. 582-590.

[2] "Τάνταλος καὶ ἄλλα ἔχων ἐστὶν ἀλγεινὰ ὁπόσα "Ομηρος ἐπ' αὐτῷ πεποίηκεν —ἐπὶ δὲ αὐτοῖς πρόσεστιν οἱ καὶ τὸ ἐκ τοῦ ἐπηρτημένου λίθου δεῖμα."—PAUS. x. 28. And—

"Πολύγνωτος μὲν δῆλός ἐστιν ἐπακολουθήσας τῷ 'Αρχιλόχου λόγῳ."—PAUS. x. This addition brings to our mind—

  "Quid memorem Lapithas, Ixiona, Pirithoumque
   quos super atra silex jam jam lapsura, cadentique
   imminet assimilis."—VIRG. Æn. vi. 600-601.

As we read through the long detailed account of Pausanias we hope that, at the end, he will take some general survey, characterise the work of Polygnotus, and unfold the plan and sequence of the vast design. But no; his account closes with perhaps the vaguest, tritest, and most unsatisfactory sentence ever written by careless traveller. Great though the debt we owe him, we cannot but read with vexation,—" Such is the number of subjects depicted, and such the suitability (or beauty) of their portrayal in the picture of the Thasian artist."[1]

Much greater would have been our vexation had our purpose been purely artistic, not in the main mythological; it would then have been our harassing and most perplexing task to determine with as much precision as possible what Pausanias meant by such ever-recurring phrases as "near to this" (τοῦ πλησίον); "above what we have described" (ἀνωτέρω τῶν κατειλεγμένων); "next in order" (ἐφεξῆς μετά); "in the lower part of the picture" (εἰς τὸ ἄνω τῆς γραφῆς); and a host of others. This troublesome task we are spared. For mythological purposes it is enough that Pausanias distinctly names the persons represented, and that, by the help of the modern artist, some rough notion of their relative juxtaposition is clearly before our eye. Without dealing in refinements as to each particular group, we must now determine broadly the significance of these persons.

Those figures which appear in the Homeric Hades require, I think, no apology for their presence here. Such are nine of the thirteen fair women—Iphimedeia, Ariadne, Phædra, Tyro, Eriphyle, Chloris, Prokris, Clymene, Megara.

[1] "τοσαύτη μὲν πλῆθος καὶ εὐπρεπείας ἐς τοσοῦτόν ἐστιν ἤκουσα ἡ τοῦ Θασίου γράφη."—PAUS. x. 28.

We are only surprised to miss the remaining four, Epikaste, Antiope, Leda, and Alkmene. In their place we have the two Pandarids, also Auge and Thyia, though I do not believe the coincidence of numbers to be intentional. The groups of Greek and Asiatic heroes are natural and indispensable in a picture which was the counterpart of another design called the Iliou persis; on the right hand of the Lesche would be Trojan and Greek in the world above; on the left Trojan and Greek in the world below. The group of Odysseus and Teiresias was necessitated by the very title of the picture—"The descent of Odysseus into Hades." Certain other figures are present probably on complimentary grounds. Tellis and Cleobeia are doubtless in part a tribute to the painter's own island, Thasos; Pelias and Schedios represent their native Phocis. The opposite ends of the picture, the prelude and the close, are occupied by groups whose significance is mainly religious. The presence of such groups is natural in a painting which decorates a hall of the temple at Delphi, the great seat of the cult of the Dorian Apollo. Vice we see punished, virtue rewarded,—specially such vices as consist in the violation of the laws of natural affection and in contempt for things sacred to the gods. The code of Apollo was a simple one: it prescribed dutiful reverence of son to father, wife to husband, all men to the gods. Among the blessed we have therefore the two young lovers who reverence their mystic cista; Antilochus, model of filial piety; Protesilaos, of conjugal fidelity; Achilles and Patroclus, of faithful friendship. Among the accursed we have a son who slew his father, a king who oppressed his subjects, a criminal who did violence to a goddess on her way to a sacred shrine.

The question has been asked more than once, What was the fundamental purport of the picture, and which in consequence is its central group? Did Polygnotus desire to realise the conception of the national poet, or to embellish local tradition, or to allegorise and embody a theory of the future state? Was his intent, in a word, poetic, historic, or doctrinally religious? Such a question appears to me to imply a sharp differentiation of modes of thought which is thoroughly and exclusively modern; we miss in these modern days much of the mutual significance of poetry, history, and religion, because we will put asunder what God and nature have joined together. We cannot, I think, look fairly from end to end of the picture of Polygnotus without feeling that the three elements are united and harmonised in proportions so subtle as to defy analysis; we may say, indeed, and we do say, that, compared with the Esquiline wall-painting, the design of Polygnotus is the more religious and the more historical of the two, the less purely mythological; but that is from its more comprehensive and complete character, not from any one-sided doctrinal emphasis.

In describing the two pictures, we have noted incidentally their chief points of contrast: it may be profitable to recapitulate. In our Esquiline landscape the human interest of the picture all centred in one group; in the Lesche picture it is dispersed among many. In the landscape the ghosts are absorbed in anxiety to have speech with Odysseus; in the Lesche picture they pursue their own occupation with marked *insouciance*. In the landscape each shade is but one of a throng, uncharacterised, except occasionally, by name; in the Lesche picture not only is each inscribed, but in most cases each is further marked out by some characteristic attribute or gesture. Lastly, in the landscape, all the persons presented (with the exception of the Danaides) are Homeric; in the Lesche picture Polygnotus drew his heroes and heroines not only from Homer, but from other Cyclic poems — the Minyas, the Lesser Iliad, the Nostoi, the Iliou-persis, the Cypria, also from logographoi (λογῶν συνθέται) and other sources unknown even to Pausanias. These points of contrast are, we at once see, closely interdependent; they result in the main from the different artistic conditions of the centuries which respectively produced the two designs. Ability to conceive and capacity to execute act and react upon each other. The idea of a large and lovely landscape, with a group of human actors centred in the foreground, but accessory in effect, would have been a notion foreign to the mind of Polygnotus, its execution impossible to his hand. He could indicate a tree, a bit of water,—any symbol of locale; but with his four simple colours,[1]—black, white, red, yellow, with little if any forecast of the perspective of Agatharcus, or the chiaroscuro of Apollodorus,—how could he, had he wished it, have brought nature into a predominance which would have seemed to him unnatural? His triumphs—and splendid triumphs he won—were in the higher field of humanity; his it was to open the sealed lips, to lighten the darkened eyes, to relax the rigorous muscles.[2] That his design

[1] Empedokles says incidentally that the painters of his time used four colours, and by their mixture (just as nature by her four elements) produced all the desired effects. We wonder how the *blue-black* demon of Eurynomus was compounded,—how shadowy were the rushes, and how solid the phantom fishes! The lovely, though severe, effect of these four colours may be seen in such vase-paintings as the "Aphrodite on the Swan" in the British Museum.

[2] Pliny says of him that he first began "os adaperire, dentes ostendere, voltum ab antiquo rigore variare."

was strictly architectonic, his arrangement carefully balanced —that he obeyed every ancient and honoured canon of composition—we may feel sure; but to him law became ordered freedom, and, within the limits of even hieratic rigour, he knew how to give utterance to the wider ethics of idealised human character ($ἦθος$).

However fascinating may be the attempted reconstruction of that which is for ever lost, it is a relief to quit the unknown for the known,—to leave the fancied picture of Polygnotus and turn to the actual vase-painting, though by an inferior hand and of later date. In it we may expect to see, not indeed actual copies of the motives of particular Lesche groups, though that is possible, but some faint image, some reflection, or perhaps—for time's atmosphere is dense—some refraction of the mighty painter's thought.

In Plate 33 we have a design from a vase now in the museum at Carlsruhe. In the centre is the palace of Hades, a splendid building, rich with costly decoration. Within we see Pluton himself, with his sceptre in his hand; to the left of him Persephone, also holding a sceptre, and seated on a richly ornamented chair. By her side stands an Erinys, bearing two flaming torches; she is youthful, and wears the conventional dress of the Erinys—in late art that of a maiden huntress,—buskins on her feet, and a wild beast's skin girt about her. Lower down on the picture, and considerably to the left, are two more Erinues in similar garb; the standing one is winged and bears a twisted snake on her left arm; her companion, who has a snake, is seated on a wild beast's skin. Both are in graceful attitudes of careless repose; for a while they cease to discharge

Pl. 33.

their dread functions, and why ? The familiar words return to us—

> " quin ipsae stupuere domus, atque intima leti
> Tartara, caeruleosque implexae crinibus angues
> Eumenides ; "

and turning again to our picture, we see why upon the "high halls of Dis" has fallen this calm unwonted,—

> " Necnon Threicius longa cum veste sacerdos
> Obloquitur numeris septem discrimina vocum,
> Jamque eadem digitis iam pectine pulsat eburno."

Surely some such figure must have met the Roman poet's eyes. Here we have the long Thracian priestly garment, while in the picture of Polygnotus Pausanias observed with surprise the mystic bard in simple Hellenic dress.

To the right of the picture is another listening group. Midway between a youth and a maiden stands a woman-figure holding an empty jar; perhaps, though for the storeage of his Formian wine Horace used most likely a rude unpainted Læstrygonian amphora, he may have seen a vase from Hellas on which some such design was depicted, for he tells us—

> " stetit urna paulum
> Sicca dum grato Danai puellas
> Carmine mulces."

Who the youth and the maiden are is uncertain; they seem to be happy souls, like Tellis and Cleobeia, unpunished in the world below.

Descending to the lower plane, we see to the left the figure of Sisyphus, already twice familiar. For the centre group, the youth with the club straining to hold the three-headed Cerberus, we turn back to Homer, and hear Odysseus tell of the "phantom of mighty Heracles." "About him was there a clamour of the dead, as it were fowls flying every way in fear, and he, like black Night, with bow uncased, and shaft upon the string, fiercely glancing around, like one in act to shoot. And about his breast was an awful belt, a baldric of gold, whereon wondrous things were wrought—bears and wild boars, and lions with flashing eyes, and strife and battles, and slaughters and manslayings. Nay, after fashioning this, never another may he fashion, whoso stored in his craft the device of this belt."[1] No Hellenic artist of Homer's days, we are now sure, could have fashioned this wondrous belt. Homer must have seen, and, with a poet's fancy, grouped, the splendid and delicate handiwork of some Phœnician craftsmen.[2] On our vase-painting all this magnificence of dress and circumstance is wanting. We see Herakles, not arrayed as a triumphant conqueror, who "hath to wife Hebe of the fair ankles," and sits for ever at the "banquet of the deathless gods," but still militant, toiling at the hardest of his labours. He tells his story to Odysseus.

"Son of Laertes, of the seed of Zeus, Odysseus of many devices. Ah, wretched one, dost thou too lead such a life of evil doom as I bore beneath the rays of the sun? I was the son of Zeus Cronion, yet I had trouble beyond measure, for I was subdued unto a man far worse than I. And he enjoined on me hard adventures; yea, and on a time he sent me hither to bring back the hound of hell; for he devised no harder task for me than this. I lifted the hound

[1] *Od.* xi. 604.
[2] Mr. C. T. Newton's, *Essays on Archæology,* p. 272; and Dr. Schliemann's *Discoveries at Mycenæ.*

and brought him forth from out of the house of Hades; and Hermes sped me on my way, and the gray-eyed Athene."[1]

In our picture Hermes, unmistakeable from his caduceus, speeds the hero on his way; and we should like to think that to the right the woman who lights the dark pathway with her torch is the "gray-eyed Athene;" but the dress and attributes forbid us, and we are left to suppose she is the dreadful Hecate who performs for once this friendly office. Behind her stands a female figure, of uncertain significance, possibly Alkmene.

Far less easy of determination are the figures grouped on either side in the topmost plane—a matron and two very young boys to the left, two youths on the right. The intent of these groups would be wholly obscure but for our knowledge of two other vases of very similar design; one of these fortunately has its figures inscribed. From a comparison of these we learn with certainty that the matron seated to the left is Megara, the wife of Herakles, with her two sons; and the group to the right represents Orestes and Pylades; possibly their presence indicates the vengeance that follows upon crime. The existence of these three similar vases, of which unhappily we are only able to offer one, makes it almost certain that they are copies from some great original, now lost, by some master other than Polygnotus.

Viewing the design figured in Plate 33 as a whole, it affords us an excellent specimen of the characteristics of late though still very fine ceramography. We see with regret that art, while it has attained freedom and dexterity, has

[1] *Od.* xi. 617.

lost its early severe beauty. The field is overcrowded; there is a striving after pictorial effect which is out of harmony with the tectonic conditions and limits of the vase surface. The heaping together of successive scenes, raised tier above tier, is an attempt at the perspective of distance; but it leaves the eye weary with a crowded impression very different from the restful effect of the early, simple grouping. The general treatment, too, of the draperies and accessories is over luxuriant. Witness the almost sensational splendour of the winged Erinys,[1] and the gorgeous attire of the Thracian bard. It is curious to note how Greek artists at first patiently evolved for themselves out of Phœnician complexity a simplicity truly Hellenic, and then, when perfection was attained, rapidly reverted to a complexity which became at last almost barbaric. At present that sad period of decadence still seems far away. The figures of Sisyphus, of Hermes, most of all of Herakles, while showing complete mastery of outline, are full of strength; and Cerberus shows us that a three-headed dog need be no monster.

Turning from the manner to the matter of our picture, it is evident, I think, that here, far more than in the Polygnotus picture, the presence and functions of Orpheus are emphasised. There he was depicted simply playing on his lyre "upon a certain hill,"[2] with musicians grouped

[1] These Erinys figures seem to have come much into fashion on vase-paintings, possibly in consequence of the scenic effects in the Eumenides of Æschylus. Later, we know from Demosthenes that Hades was peopled, modern fashion, with a whole crew of impersonated horrors :—"μεθ' ὧν δ' οἱ ζωγράφοι τοὺς ἀσεβεῖς ἐν Ἅιδου γράφουσι μετὰ τούτων μέτ'. Ἀρᾶς καὶ Βλασφημίας καὶ Φθόνου καὶ Στάσεως καὶ Νείκους περιέρχεται."—*Cont. Arist.* i. p. 489 (786).

[2] "ἐπὶ λόφου τινός"—a hill probably indicated by the conventional dotted lines, such as occur in our vase-picture.

around listening, as they might on earth; here he chains the attention of Pluto and Persephone, the dread gods of Hades, and the Erinues cease their work to listen. Herakles is present, perhaps, as a sort of heroic counterpart to Orpheus,—what the musician availed to do by his music the hero achieved by pure strength; but in tracing analogies in vase-painting we tread on slippery ground. Orpheus would still more certainly be the central figure of the design, could we determine more clearly that the uppermost groups have relation to Orphic mysteries and initiation; but here we must be content for the present to doubt.

Turning to Plate 34, we have another vase-painting the Orphic significance of which is unmistakeable. The design is from a large krater now in the British Museum, of presumably about the same date as our last picture (*i.e.* somewhere in the fourth or early part of the third century B.C.) Here we have no palace of Persephone; we are sure, however, that we are in the under world, for we see Cerberus; also we notice a tall slender tree, which rears its crown of leaves to the upper world, where are grouped in graceful conclave Pan and Hermes, Aphrodite and Eros; and we remember that in the picture of Polygnotus Orpheus leant against a tree. Possibly this is a reminiscence, or it may be taken direct from Homer, who tells, as we know, of the " groves of Persephone, even tall poplar trees and willows, that shed their fruit before the season."[1] Close to this tree is Orpheus; in the one hand he holds his lyre, which he reaches out to an approaching boy, with the other he restrains Cerberus, who is about to fall on the new-comer. Orpheus, we

[1] " ἄλσεα Περσεφονείης
μακραί τ' αἴγειροι καὶ ἰτέαι ὠλεσίκαρποι."—*Od.* x. 509.

remember, had power by his music to sway the hound of hell.[1] And who, we ask, is the youth who approaches, led by an older man? Surely a boy who, early instructed by his father in the mysteries of the holy religion of Orpheus, is initiated in the world above, and, dying, is welcomed by the author of his faith to the world below. The lyre is offered no doubt with reference to some ritual detail of initiation now lost to us, but this gesture seems the intelligible and natural symbol of union and complete fruition. The female figure to the right of Orpheus some have thought to be the pious mother of the boy, gone home before him; more likely it is Eurydike, though her presence here has no special significance.

We might multiply examples, but these two vase-paintings, out of a multitude which represent scenes from the lower world, will serve our purpose, namely, to see how, as time went on, the simple epic conception of Hades became transformed by complex religious associations, by the influence of creeds and doctrines, to the mysteries of which we no longer hold the clue. Our latest art monument, the Esquiline landscape in Autotype VI., we placed first, partly because it dealt with the opening scene of our myth, but chiefly because it was in spirit the most simple and Homeric. A thing so lovely in itself as this landscape we may not call *ir*religious, but it is certainly *non*-religious, the work of a man who either has no creed, or is not concerned artistically to enforce it.

In this Greek Hades we have, as we see, traces of

[1] " Cessat immanis tibi blandienti
　　　Janitor aulæ
　Cerberus."　　　　　HORAT. *Carm.* iii. 11, 14.

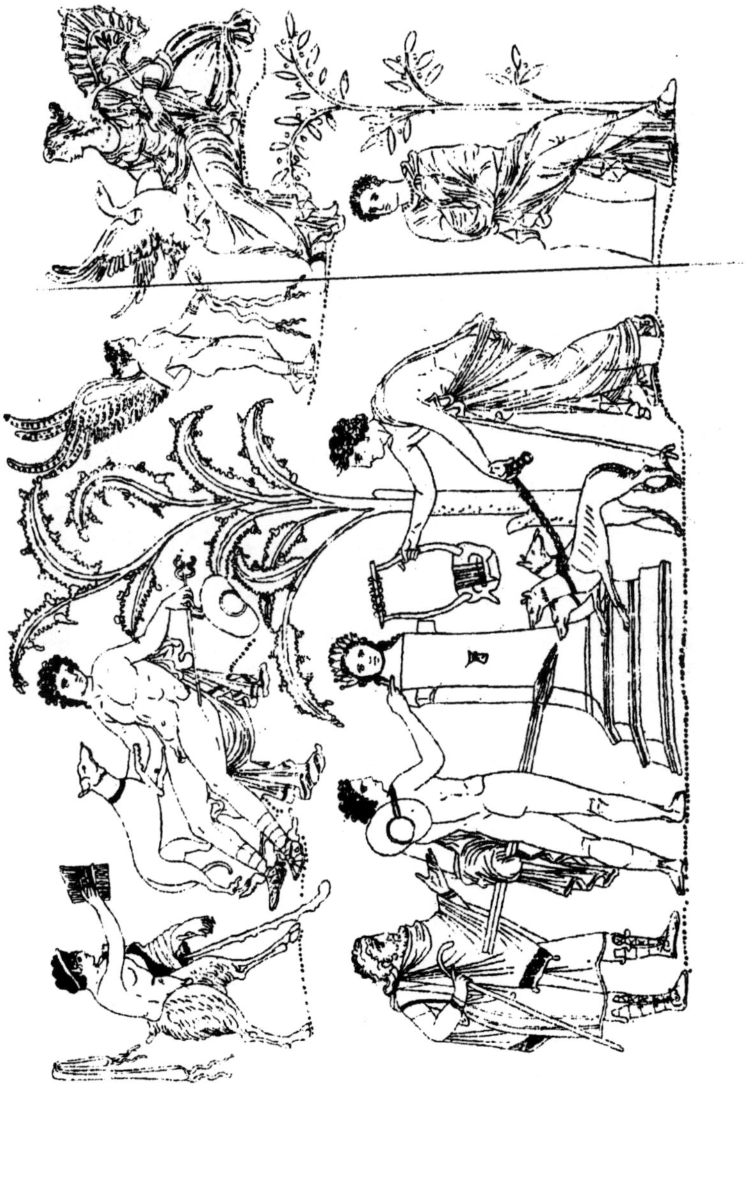

growing doctrinal mysticism; we have also the downright expression of righteous retribution which overtakes the grievous criminal; but still in the main the under world atmosphere is serene, even cheerful. We must turn now to Italy, and visit the ghosts of another, a more gloomy land, grim Etruria.

However much Etrurian conceptions were modified by the influence of the traditions of pure Greek art, there still remains about them for the most part a touch of the grotesque, the horrible. We constantly miss that Hellenic euphemism, that quick instinct for beauty and limit, which prompts the true Greek artist to conceal deformity and soften terror.

The pictures before us (in Plates 35 and 36) are from the second chamber of the Tomba dell Orco at Corneto. Of the three chambers into which the tomb is divided, one, the second, is entirely decorated with scenes from the under world. Space forbids us to give the whole, but our two examples are chosen as specially characteristic of Etrurian thought. Let us turn to Plate 35. To the right we have the Theban seer again inscribed, much the same as in the Etruscan mirror (see Plate 29), with very mysterious letters. He leans upon a staff, something of anxious weakness in his posture. He wears the long prophetic veil; his eyes are closed; his head droops slightly, with the same expression of dreamy blindness we noted in the mirror. In fact in the whole figure the pathos of blindness is very forcibly expressed. The beard and hair are luxuriant and curl softly. The colouring of the drapery is somewhat dull and austere.

In contrast to this venerable seer of sad and feeble aspect comes a figure on whom, even though inadequately painted by an Etruscan artist, we may not look without the keenest emotion,—Memnon, "goodly Memnon" the most beautiful man of all the ancient world.[1] He is inscribed MEMRUN, and he is here represented in the full glory of manhood; long curling hair falls upon his shoulders and circles his forehead. Once already we have met him in the Hades of Polygnotos. Why he now stands so near to Teiresias we cannot tell. Probably the juxtaposition is merely accidental. Both at this moment are in strange company. On either side of Teiresias are reed-like, branching trees; on the tree to the left strange pigmy black figures are climbing and clinging in every manner of grotesque, jocund attitude; one swings suspended by his hand, one swarms a branch, one stands balancing himself. Who are these strange black pigmies? we may well ask, and no certain answer can be given. Some have thought they are tiny Ethiopians, present, like the two negro boys in the Lesche picture, more clearly to identify Memnon. This seems improbable. Others recall the mighty elm Æneas saw in Hades, thronged with the clustering phantoms of vain dreams—

> "In medio ramos, annosaque brachia pandit
> Ulmus opaca, ingens; quam sedem Somnia vulgo
> Vana tenere ferunt, *foliisque sub omnibus hærent.*"
> VIRG. *Æn.* vi. 282-284.

Perhaps the most probable solution is that the pigmies are tiny souls. We know that it was the custom of Greek art to represent the soul as a tiny winged figure fluttering above the body it had left. Still we wonder to see these

---

[1] Achilles says of Eurypylus—

"κεῖνον δὴ κάλλιστον ἴδον μετὰ Μέμνονα δῖον."—*Od.* xi. 522.

Pl. 35.

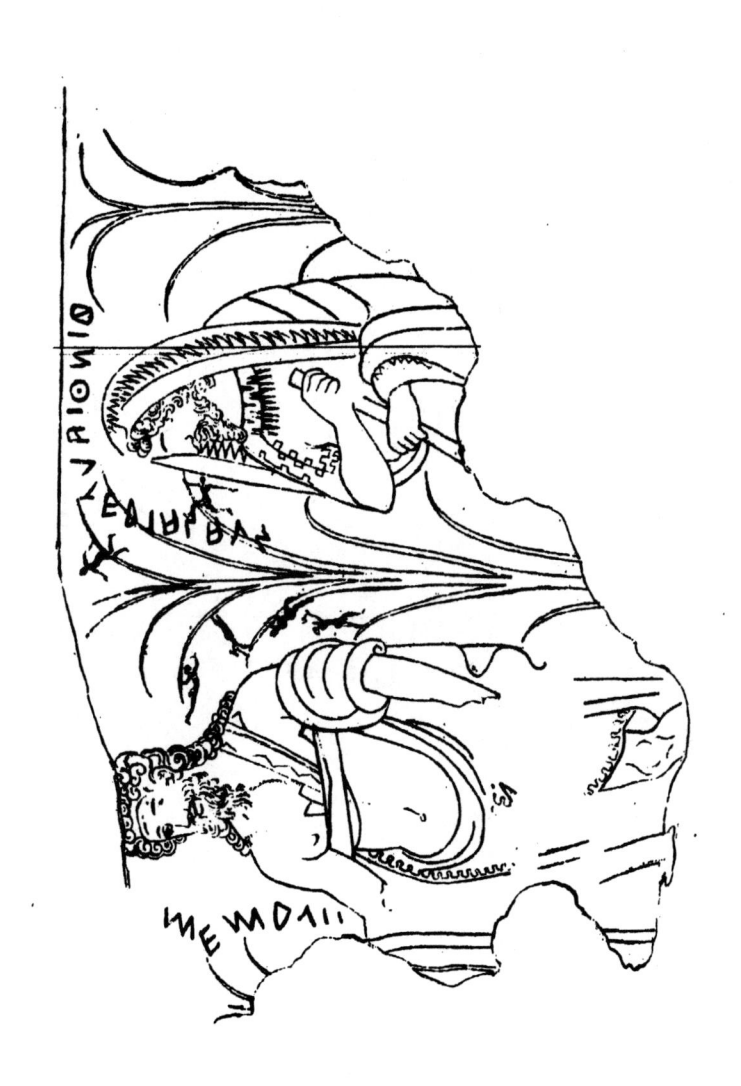

souls, if such they be, disporting themselves after the fashion of imps and gnomes. But such unseemly pranks accord not ill with the grim humour of Etrurian.

Humour, however grim, deserts us in our second Etruscan wall-picture. Turning to Plate 36, we find horror unrelieved by any lighter touch. Here we have an infernal demon of truly Etruscan pattern—a frightful shape, with open mouth to show his grinning teeth. He has great wings, and strides on holding in both his hands a large hammer. He looks like one of the "workmen" (faber) who, Plutarch tells us,[1] torture with their tools the souls of the covetous below. The flesh of this demon is of greenish hue; his nose is hooked like an eagle's beak, about his shoulders are serpents, and the fierce monster is made more beast-like by his satyr's ear. All these dreadful details are drawn with considerable force and delicacy, as if the subject were much to the artist's liking. The limbs are full and round, the muscles peculiarly well emphasised. We ask at once who the demon is. The inscription helps us but little, though it confirms what is undoubtedly the right solution. One letter only remains, the archaic equivalent of the letter X. When we read of the green flesh, the grinning teeth, at once we remember the Delphic demon Eurynomos, and our thoughts are carried still further back to the fabled shield of Herakles, on which Hesiod tells us[2] the "Keres" were

---

[1] Plutarch de sera num vindict. cap. 22.

[2] Κῆρες κυάνεαι, λευκοὺς ἀραβεῦσαι ὀδόντας,
δεινωποὶ βλοσυροί τε δαφοινοί τ' ἀπλητοί τε
δῆριν ἔχον περὶ πιπτόντων, πᾶσαι δ' ἄρ' ἵεντο
αἷμα μέλαν πιέειν· ὃν δὲ πρῶτον μεμάποιεν
κείμενον ἢ πίπτοντα νεούτατον ἀμφὶ μὲν αὐτῷ
βάλλ' ὄνυχας μεγάλους.—HESIOD, Scut., 249-254.

graven, demons worthy to be the ancestors of Eurynomos; they too were of blue-black colour, with mighty claws, and they ground their white teeth, waiting to drink the black blood of the slain. One of these same monsters was sculptured, Pausanias tells us,[1] on the chest of Cypselos.

Archaic art seems to have dealt somewhat freely in these terrible impersonations, but later Hellenic art with its euphemistic tendencies kept such horrors in the background, though still we have fantastic furies such as we have noted on our vase-painting (Plate 33). But in Etruria, the proper home of grotesque terror, all such creations found an appropriate dwelling-place. Even the harmless waterman Charon, who at worst in Hellas is somewhat churlish and uncouth, is in Etruria transformed into a minister of torture to the damned, the very monster before us. How the transformation was effected it is not easy to trace, but we have already noted that Charon has met with a similar fate in modern Hellas. Perhaps it was only for a few happy centuries, when beauty reigned supreme, that even the Greeks could resist the strong doctrinal impulse which besets mankind to people hell with horrors.

For such horrors Etruria shall suffice. Time forbids us to descend with Æneas down the easy steep of Avernus, nor may we question the tortured ghosts that dwell in Dante's *Inferno,* nor yet the devils that plot and plan in the Pandemonium of Milton. It is rash to tarry so long in Hades, lest the dim uncertain twilight baffle and daze us,

---

[1] τῶν δὲ Οἰδίποδος παίδων Πολυνείκει πεπτωκότι ἐς γόνυ ἔπεισιν Ἐτεοκλῆς. τοῦ Πολυνείκους δὲ ὄπισθεν ἔστηκεν ὀδόντας τε ἔχουσα οὐδὲν ἡμερωτέρους θηρίου, καὶ οἱ καὶ τῶν χειρῶν εἰσιν ἐπικαμπεῖς οἱ ὄνυχες ἐπίγραμμα δὲ ἐπ' αὐτῇ εἶναι φασι Κῆρα.—PAUS. v. 17.

Pl. 36.

and we behold no longer clearly the light of the upper world. Let us remember the caution of the simple-hearted Odysseus: "And pale fear gat hold of me lest the high goddess Persephone should send me the head of the Gorgon, that dread monster from out of Hades."

The light of the upper world streams in again as we read, "Straightway then I went to the ship, and bade my men mount the vessel and loose the hawsers. So speedily they went on board, and sat upon the benches, and the wave of the flood bore the bark down the stream of Oceanus, we rowing first, and afterwards the fair wind was our convoy."[1]

[1] *Od.* xi. 635.

This is the end of this publication.

Any remaining blank pages are for our book binding requirements and are blank on purpose.

To search thousands of interesting publications like this one, please remember to visit our website at:

http://www.kessinger.net

Printed in the United States
54110LVS00003B/4